Léon Paul Fargue: Droga

Nemohu zapomenout na počet jednoho rána

        V Alexandra Park

když jsem byl úplně spojen sbělými holuby
byli bílí jak sníh

On pán vehohovorsha sherre drogu zva-

        nou arkein

the drug of art
of modest small old surrealistic art.

The Drug of Art

by Ivan Blatný

Ugly Duckling Presse
Eastern European Poets Series #15

Ivan Blatný
The Drug of Art: Selected Poems
© 2007 by Ugly Duckling Presse and Veronika Tuckerová

Translations © Matthew Sweney, Alex Zucker, Justin Quinn,
       Veronika Tuckerová and Anna Moschovakis
Foreword © Josef Škvorecký
Afterword © Antonín Petruželka
Introduction © Veronika Tuckerová
"About this edition" © Antonín Petruželka, Veronika Tuckerová

Cover image: *Two Ladies*, muchláž, 1985 © Galerie ART Chrudim for Jiří Kolář, used by permission
Manuscript images and scans © Literární archiv Památníku národního písemnictví
Working scans provided by Bartoloměj Petruželka
Cover design, book design and typesetting: Macabea Can Type
Cover printing: Polyprint & Design

Distributed to the trade (through Zephyr Press) by Consortium [www.cbsd.com]
ISBN 9780939010912
Distributed to the trade by Small Press Distribution [www.spdbooks.org]
ISBN 9781933254166

       Library of Congress Cataloging-in-Publication Data

Blatný, Ivan, 1919-1990
[Selections. English and Czech. 2007]
The drug of art / by Ivan Blatný ; translated by Matthew Sweney ... [et al.] ; edited and with and introduction by Veronika Tuckerov. -- 1st ed.
       p. cm. -- (Eastern European poets series ; #15)
English and Czech.
Includes bibliographical references.
ISBN 978-0-939010-91-2 (pbk. : alk. paper) -- ISBN 978-1-933254-16-6 (pbk. : alk. paper)
I. Sweney, Matthew. II. Tuckerova, Veronika. III. Title.
PG5039.12.L28A2 2007
891.8'635--dc22

              2007021530

The Drug of Art is Eastern European Poets Series #15
Project editor, Eastern European Poets Series: Anna Moschovakis
Series editors, Eastern European Poets Series: Matvei Yankelevich and Genya Turovskaya

First Edition 2007

       Ugly Duckling Presse
       The Old American Can Factory
       232 Third Street #E002
       Brooklyn NY 11215
       www.uglyducklingpresse.org

This project is supported in part by an award from the
National Endowment for the Arts.

This project is supported in part by a grant from the
New York State Council on the Arts, a state agency.

IVAN BLATNÝ

The Drug of Art

TRANSLATED BY MATTHEW SWENEY, JUSTIN QUINN,
ALEX ZUCKER, VERONIKA TUCKEROVÁ & ANNA MOSCHOVAKIS

EDITED AND WITH AN INTRODUCTION BY VERONIKA TUCKEROVÁ

Foreword

IVAN BLATNÝ WAS one of the poets of my youth. Most of all I liked to read his *Melancholy Walks*. After the coup d'etat we learned that Blatný, who was on a research fellowship in the West, would not come back. After some time we learned that he had lost his sanity and was in an asylum.

About thirty years later, when my wife and I were in exile in Canada, and Zdena had founded the publishing house Sixty-Eight Publishers, we received a letter from Miss Meacham in England. She wrote that she was in touch with a patient at the local institute for the mentally ill in Clacton-on-Sea, who wrote poems in a language that she did not comprehend. Some people in London had told her about our publishing house.

Naturally, I realized who the poet was and replied to Miss Meacham that we would be interested in the poems. After some time, a voluminous package arrived full of various papers and scraps, medical prescriptions, and pages from a notebook, with poems on their reverse sides, in a handwriting which was often not easy to decipher. Since I was very busy at that time with our publishing house, I sent the package to my friend, the poet Antonín Brousek, requesting that he edit a collection if he found the poems any good. Brousek responded enthusiastically, and after a while, he sent a manuscript of poems that he had selected and transcribed. He named the collection *Old Addresses*. I read the manuscript and shared Brousek's enthusiasm. We typeset the book; around that time, someone in Prague was sending me a series of beautiful postcards by Kamil Lhoták, who was my friend and who used to be a friend of Ivan Blatný's; we used one for the cover, and the result was a handsome volume of beautiful modern poetry. Miss Meacham then wrote to me that it was our book (we sent Blatný a few copies) which had finally persuaded the attending physicians that Blatný was a real poet, not just a madman who believed that he was a poet. They allotted him a private room and a typewriter so that he could write.

Brousek then edited another collection of poems written in four languages, called *Bixley Remedial School*.

I personally met Blatný only once, unfortunately on a bad day. I spoke mainly with Miss Meacham, Blatný only sat and didn't speak; I don't know whether he listened. He was indeed seriously mentally ill. But on his good days he still knew how to write beautiful poems.

I continued to correspond with Miss Meacham after 1989.

And that's about all.

—Josef Škvorecký
(translated by Veronika Tuckerová)

The Drug of Art

Table of Contents

ANOTHER POETICAL LESSON:
UNCOLLECTED POEMS

AFTERWORD by Antonín Petruželka

NOTES

ACKNOWLEDGMENTS

Introduction

A POET DISAPPEARS

I first came into contact with Ivan Blatný's poems in the mid-1980s in Prague. The book was *Bixley Remedial School* (*Pomocná škola Bixley*), published in *samizdat* in 1982.[1] On the cover of the slim volume was a striking photograph of a frail man in a checkered jacket. The title seemed exotic to me; I later learned that it referred to the Bixley Ward-Warren House of St. Clement's Hospital in Ipswich, England—the mental institution where Blatný had been residing since 1977. In Czechoslovakia at that time, this *samizdat* edition was one of the very few signs of the poet's existence.[2] Blatný's poetry had been blacklisted since 1948; apart from a few exceptions in the 1960s, his poems had not been published in his own country.[3] In the early 1980s, with his exile exceeding three decades, only the poet's family and a close circle of friends knew his whereabouts.

Blatný's life and work were marked by the social and political upheavals in Czechoslovakia in the second half of the twentieth century. Born in 1919 in Brno, he was among the most talented poets of his generation, admired for the musicality of his verse; he published four volumes of poetry and two books of children's verse before he turned thirty. In the spring of 1948, shortly after the Communist coup d'etat, Blatný left for London along with the poet Jiří Kolář and the writer Arnošt Vaněček on a cultural-exchange trip financed by the British Council. On his first night in England, he announced on the BBC that he would not return home, adding a few sentences in which he criticized conditions under the new regime. (Communist newspapers reported that he claimed a "cold terror" had been brought by the Communists to his native land[4] and that poets were being forced by the Communist Party to make "art for the people."[5]) Blatný was immediately stripped of his citizenship and condemned in the Communist press. It is jarring today to read the words with which his fellow poets, including his friends, denounced Blatný, accusing him of pettiness, cowardice, lies and betrayal. "The poet Ivan Blatný is dead forever in Czech literature,"[6] reads the official declaration of the Committee of the Club of Young Writers, signed by, among others, the critic Jindřich Chalupecký and the poet Kamil Bednář. Similarly, the Syndicate of Czech Writers—the official organization on whose behalf Blatný had traveled to England—disassociated itself from

him: Its declaration stated that Blatný, by his "lying and scandalizing declarations about the conditions in Czechoslovakia…expelled himself from our national community." The poet Kamil Bednář quoted from the patriotic verses of the nationalistically minded poet Viktor Dyk, in which the "voice of the country" implores: "If you leave me, I won't die; if you leave me, you will die."[7] The volume and quality of Blatný's poetry from his years in exile demonstrate just how wrong these provincial prophecies were—while his art continued to develop, Czech official poetry degraded itself in the hands of propaganda officials.

No scholarly biography of Blatný has been written, and numerous questions about the facts of his life in exile remain unanswered. Any published version of his life story runs the risk of erring in one of two directions—either by inadvertently perpetuating an often-repeated and (at best) reductive legend, or by engaging in speculations that complicate that legend but are difficult or impossible to verify. The uncertainty extends even to the most basic reasons for Blatný's extended hospitalization. While some reports mention specific diagnoses and severe symptoms,[8] a quite different story has it that Blatný was primarily seeking refuge, rather than therapy, in mental hospitals. Blatný certainly did write, in a number of poems, of a fear of being deported. And evidence exists of the Czechoslovak secret police's interest in Blatný. In the late 1950s, the poet was given the code name Salamander (*Mlok*) and an agent was sent to inquire about his plans for returning to Czechoslovakia. If Blatný had agreed to return, regime officials planned to use him for propaganda— their hope, recorded in the secret police files, was that after experiencing the "conditions of material scarcity" of his life in exile, the poet's political allegiences would have shifted and he would be willing to "exert influence on workers in cultural areas."[9] (Apparently, Blatný did not change his mind about Communist rule. In an interview conducted in St. Clement's Hospital by the writer and journalist Jürgen Serke which Serke incorporated in an article for the journal *Stern* in 1981, Blatný asserts that he "did not make a mistake" by emigrating, that the Socialism he once supported had "turned into a horrible, hollow word." He also expands on his fear of capture: "The thought that the Communists could kidnap me became an *idée fixe* of mine and I was terribly afraid. The fear stopped only when I found a refuge in the institution.")[10]

Despite the questions that remain open, a rough chronology of events from the poet's life after 1948 can be sketched. For the purposes of this introduction, I aim to present only the most incontrovertable elements of the generally accepted chronology, those verified by the accounts of Blatný's editors and family members.

In 1948, only months after settling in England, Blatný was briefly hospitalized for mental illness, first in London and then at Claybury Hospital, in Essex. That same fall, he was declared dead on Czechoslovak radio.[11] From 1948 to 1954, he worked on and off as a journalist, collaborating at times with the BBC and Radio Free Europe. He then spent the years from 1954 until his death in 1990 living at various institutions: first at Claybury again; then from 1963 to 1977 at the House of Hope in Ipswich; and then until 1985 at St. Clement's Hospital, also in Ipswich. He spent the last five years of his life at the Edensor nursing home, in Clacton-on-Sea. A comparison of the Foreword and Afterword to this edition will attest to the disagreements about the exiled poet's psychological state. Serke's conclusion was that Blatný's criticism of Communist Czechoslovakia and his reflections on his own situation amounted to the "clear words of a man who has a clear mind."[12] The publisher Martin Reiner (formerly Pluháček), who interviewed Blatný in 1989, offers a more nuanced view of the émigré's condition: "Documents from later times indicate that he was not so ill as not to be able to live, in due time, as anybody else. According to medical reviews he could. But in reality a so-called normal life was impossible for the aging melancholic of the Pisárky alleys. The last ground on which Blatný could stride was that of his inner self, filled with rainy images of his native Brno."[13]

Blatný hardly wrote in the 1950s and 1960s,[14] but that fallow period was followed by a prolific one during which he "filled several hundred copybooks."[15] Many of his manuscripts were presumably lost, discarded by hospital personnel who believed them the worthless scribblings of a psychiatric patient. On a recent trip to Brno I met with Blatný's cousin Jan Šmarda. He recalled visiting his cousin at the House of Hope in Ipswich in 1969, and showed me the postcard-collages that Kolář used to send to Blatný.[16] He also recalled how, after Blatný's transfer in 1977 to St. Clement's, a fortunate series of events led to the preservation of at least some of his manuscripts. A nurse from Ipswich named Frances Meacham was visiting a friend in Czechoslovakia and met Vladimír Bařina, a poet who knew Blatný, by pure chance in Brno. Bařina put Meacham

in touch with Šmarda, who asked her to keep an eye on the poet; for about ten years she did more than that, supplying Blatný with paper and storing his manuscripts in a garbage container, bought for the purpose, which she kept in her garage.[17] She convinced the asylum's staff to allow Blatný to write poetry as the "occupational" part of his therapy (as opposed to crafting lampshades). In 1979, Blatný put together a collection of poems, which he titled *Bixley Remedial School*. A copy of that manuscript made its way to Prague (via Jiří Kolář in Paris) in 1981 and was published there, in *samizdat*, in 1982 under the imprint KDM. Meanwhile, a different collection had been selected and edited by the Czech emigré poet Antonín Brousek from among some of Blatný's manuscript pages sent by Meacham to exiled Czech writer and publisher Josef Škvorecký in Canada. That book, titled *Old Addresses* (*Stará bydliště*), was published in 1979 in Toronto by Sixty-Eight Publishers, the imprint under which Škvorecký was printing Czech and Slovak books that could not be published in Czechoslovakia. Škvorecký's press put out two poetry collections resulting from Blatný's time in exile: *Old Addresses* in 1979 and a book called *Bixley Remedial School* (also edited by Brousek, and significantly different from the *samizdat* version) in 1987.[18]

The *samizdat* version of *Bixley* contains a number of poems in which Blatný uses several languages. The last lines of one called "Leon-Paul Fargue: A Drug" read:

> On pán všeho tvorstva stvořil drogu zvanou artein[*]
> the drug of art
> of modest small old surrealistic art.

The "drug of art" may refer to the youthful enchantments of Blatný's first books, *Lady Morning Star* (*Paní Jitřenka*, 1940) and *Melancholy Walks* (*Melancholické procházky*, 1941). Written much later in Blatný's life, these lines contain an echo of those enchantments, inflected with the irony of distance.

"POET OF ONE LANGUAGE"

With the end of Communist censorship in 1989, Blatný's poetry began to reappear in Czechoslovakia. The first book of his to be republished, in 1990, was his 1941 collection, *Melancholy Walks*. (Originally the title had been *Brno Elegies* [*Brněnské elegie*], but Blatný agreed to change it to facilitate the book's publication—at the time the publishers feared

---

[*] "He the Lord of all creatures created the drug called artaine." (An image of the manuscript of this poem appears as the frontispiece for this book.)

that *Brno Elegies*, with its potential to be construed as resentful of the Nazi occupation, would not pass the censors.)[19] Reissues of *Old Addresses* and *Bixley Remedial School* followed soon after.

Reading these books in the early 1990s, I was drawn to the nostalgic mood and the melody of the *Elegies*, which also characterize many of the poems in Blatný's first exilic book, *Old Addresses*. Reminiscences play a major role in the sonnets from that book, in which the poet, who would never return to his homeland, recalls old friends, poets and painters, but also places, football players and various facts from his grammar and biology classes. Brno is strongly present. In "Cigarette," the poet returns to places he used to visit—here, in Justin Quinn's translation, he follows the blue smoke of his cigarette back to Brno:

> Blue smoke I blew out and blue smoke now floats
> to your Pisárky. I think I'm back in the woods.
> Once more, a Brno tramcar takes me there.
>
> We're going through the trees. We're swinging round
> the Expo and beyond the football ground
> to the cemetery, and girls wave in the air.

But I was also struck by the originality of Blatný's multilingual poems in *Bixley Remedial School*—the book I'd seen a decade earlier when it circulated in *samizdat* in Prague. In these poems, Blatný switches freely from Czech to English, French and German, all within a single poem and sometimes even within a line, as if the languages were all part of one primary or originary language. His own bilingual experience— first in the circle of his family (his grandmother was German), then while living in England—naturally found expression in associations that transcended linguistic borders and limitations. Sometimes, Blatný looks for a word in English to name a plant or a bird that he knows in Czech ("Linnet je konopka warbler je pěnice"*) or searches for Czech words to translate a more obscure English word ("granáty, garnets, české polodrahokamy ze severních Čech"†). He seems to delight in inventing word-plays in his adopted language—"the bumble-bee may be also called humble-bee"—and sometimes simply places corresponding words from several languages together: "Die Sonne, sun, el sol."[20]

---

* "linnet is konopka warbler is pěnice"
† "garnets, garnets, czech semi-precious stones from north Bohemia"

Often the friction between languages is at the very center of a poem, as in "Misspelled," which starts with the poet pondering a spelling mistake he has made in English:

> So restoration is not spelled *au*
> I spelled it so thinking of the czech word restaurace
> to restore
> and go with a lady to the Room
> like a unicorn in the mirror
> all naked in the mirrors
> so that I could see the blood trickling.

This poem is sparked by Blatný's realization that his mother tongue, Czech, has interfered with his command of English, as the Czech spelling of "restaurant" (*restaurace*) makes its way into the etymologically related (but semantically distinct) English word "restoration." The associations proceed from there, following a surrealist-tinged string of images in which the bodily and the mythical are united with the aid of a mirror.

The trilingual poem "The drifter sleeps in the meadow" starts in Czech but switches abruptly to English in the second line:

> Budižkničemu se toulá po ulicích města[*]
> always under pressure of the moral institutes

The third line continues in English, but in the fourth line Blatný translates the word *louky* ("meadows") into the German *die Wiesen*:

> But he won't go to a borstal
> louky die Wiesen na něj čekají za městem[†]

The next line is inspired by the word *Wiesen*:

> Wie sen jak sen how a dream
> zbytečná otázka
> stejně si nemohu nic pamatovat.

Blatný splits *Wiesen* into two parts, *Wie* and *sen*, thus deriving the German word *wie* ("how") and the Czech word *sen*, ("dream"). He then translates those words into English, in a kind of chain reaction: "Wie sen jak sen how a dream." Blatný ponders the "useless question" (*zbytečná otázka*) he arrived at by translating *Wie sen* literally into

---

[*]"The good for nothing wanders the city streets"
[†]"meadows die Wiesen await him outside of the city"

"how a dream." (His only answer is the tossed-off dismissal of the last line: "anyway I can't remember a thing.")

While there is no clear rule as to how Blatný employs the languages in his arsenal, it's often the case that his memory conjures up a word in Czech, while he typically describes his contemporary life and immediate surroundings in English: "I have now two pens and plenty of papers."[21] His other languages are called upon more rarely, with French appearing, for example, only in the title of "La verre." The last two stanzas of that poem read:

> Translate me into english
> I want to be read by Valentine Penrose
>
> In the book it is Petorose and spoils the rhythm
> Brousku, buďte příště opatrnější.

This poem, in which Blatný contemplates the editions of his various collections, has a French title, but is written in English—apart from the last line, in which the poet admonishes, in Czech, Antonín Brousek (the editor of his book *Old Addresses*) for wrongly spelling the name of the French Surrealist poet Valentine Penrose in the poem "Names": "Brousek, next time be more careful."

Blatný did occasionally address his multilingual practice within his poems. In a poem from *Bixley*, he writes:

> Jsem jenom básník jednoho jazyka
> ale miluji cizojazyčné vložky
> bras dessus bras dessous*
> there is a remote chance that I'll win the Prix Nobel for literature[22]

The first two lines, above, translate as "I am only a poet of one language / but I love foreign insertions." Taken at face value, the first part of this statement seems at odds with the substantial number of poems Blatný wrote that were essentially multilingual, as well as several written entirely or almost entirely in English. And Antonín Petruželka, a Blatný scholar and one of the editors of the *samizdat* edition of *Bixley Remedial School*, has argued that Blatný's use of languages other than Czech is no mere embellishment, that through his multilingual work the poet "liberated poetry from its monoglotic

---

* "arm on top arm below"

foundation."[23] But Blatný's love of "insertions" *is* plainly evident throughout his work, and a poetics of collage already is apparent in his early poems, which are peppered with quotations from other poets. Zbyněk Hejda, another of the editors of the *samizdat* version of *Bixley*, sees in the quotations from Apollinaire and Desnos in *Brno Elegies /Melancholy Walks* the seeds of a poetics that "would come to full flowering in the final phase of his œuvre."[24] Blatný's increased interest in collage is evident in the collections from his middle period, *This Night* (*Tento večer*, 1945) and *In Search of Present Time* (*Hledání přítomného času*, 1947), which employ a markedly different poetics from that apparent in the *Elegies*. Moving away from the lyricism of his earlier work, these poems are written in an often highly fragmented free verse, with a less unified, less emphatic voice. Blatný's lines and stanzas become expansive, thanks in part to frequent lists and the use of parataxis: In the poems from *This Night*, incongruous linguistic fragments, including shopping lists and recipes, are placed side by side on a line, without punctuation, in a composition that is more spatial than grammatical. The poem "Small Variation" includes a list of things lying on a table; here, as translated by Matthew Sweney, the list is broken down into a taxonomy of everyday objects:

> Thursday 8 pm. On the table:
> Newspapers, cigarettes, tobacco, knife, and lamp.
> Newspapers: *Papandreu, Pierlot.*
> Furniture: Divan, ornamented credenza.

In anticipation of later poems, another from this collection, "Fifth," includes a line in German and a word in French. As poetic principle, collage only becomes more pronounced in Blatný's multilingual exilic poems: In one, Blatný declares, "Chci dělat koláže, chci stále vypůjčovat / je zase éra citátů." ("I want to make collages, I always want to borrow / it is again the era of quotations.")[25] In the multilingual poems, the various languages themselves become elements to be borrowed from their original context and reused "as is" in new ones. These poems also include names of painters, poets, and towns, facts from textbooks and names of paintings, as well as quotations from Blatný's own earlier poems and bits of information from daily life. As collage becomes more dominant, it works to extend (if not supplant) the more conventionally figured nostalgia expressed in the *Elegies*, as elements from the present and the past are reunited on the page.

ISOLATION IN CONTEXT

Despite the break suggested by the events of 1948 and the isolated life Blatný led in England, his poetics is marked by continuity rather than disjunction and retains its link to Czech poetry. The "profound, inner continuity" from the young poet to the older one was emphatically pointed out by Brousek, who read Blatný's poetry from the 1970s as "self-confirmation" and a testament that "it is possible to preserve one's own identity, remain in unity with oneself," even in the difficult conditions that exile presents to a poet. According to Brousek, Blatný reached maturity in his exilic poetry, which—in the selection that Brousek made for *Old Addresses*—presents a synthesis of Poetism, Surrealism, and the "existential civilism of Group 42 [*Skupina 42*]," the three dominant styles of modern Czech poetry.[26]

Blatný's frequent references to the poets of Poetism and Surrealism (whether of French or Czech provenance), as well as to his beloved painters Toyen, Hudeček and Lhoták, attest to his allegiances to these movements. It is the emphasis on urban landscape, on the everyday and the banal, present throughout his work, that links Blatný to Group 42. A circle of painters and poets founded in 1942 around the critic Jindřich Chalupecký, and including Blatný and Kolář,[27] Group 42 rejected the Surrealist emphasis on what lies *beyond* reality, and called for a return to an unmediated vision *of* reality, for a shift from metaphoric expression to direct naming: The artist, they said, must return to his immediate reality, the city. Chalupecký evokes Charlie Chaplin, American poets, and the photography of Eugène Atget as expressions of what he calls the "mythology of modern man," or the "world in which we live." He writes, "The reality of the modern painter and poet is the city: its people, its pavements, lamp posts, store signs, houses, stairwells, flats."[28] Group 42 sought to establish a lineage with English and American writers, including T.S. Eliot, Henry Miller, and James Joyce, rather than with the French poets, as was typical for modern Czech poetry. Blatný's poems "Second" and "Third" from *This Night* enact that desire, drawing directly from the work of Langston Hughes and attesting to the poet's interest in American poetry, the modern city, jazz, and music halls.[29] The long poem, "Terrestris"—with its invocation of the witch Terrestris, a seductive personification of death and life "with bloody lips, with smashed teeth, infected by the larvae of Gypsy moths and bark beetles"—takes on darker tones, quite

different from the enchanted lyricism of the younger Blatný. But even this epic poem, with its departure from the landscape of the everyday, retains its link to Group 42; its speaker is a walker who observes the witch (an adversary as well as the object of his desire), "how she walks between trees and columns and fences and antennas"—a grotesque figure hobbling through a grotesque urban landscape.

A similar observant walker appears in Blatný's 1947 prose poem "The Game" in the figure of the Passerby, who dreams that he is traveling with his long-deceased mother to the other side of "the Curtain." At the border he is subjected to a trial, the nature and meaning of which he doesn't know, to a game the rules of which he doesn't understand. Still, the Passerby has "made up his mind to play it out to the end." A closing section in verse takes us back to the reality of the city, as the poet-narrator reappears four floors above the street, watching the Passerby and describing the scene from above.

In order to play the game to the end, the Passerby has to "volunteer" to put his leg between two giant, dull blades capable of crushing it. But when the poet-narrator returns in the closing lines, it is to renounce the game; for that, he is ready to submit to the test himself, to put his own leg on the block, but "the other way round." This time, the act of voluntary submission is folded into lines that directly address the task of poetry. A poetic manifesto of a sort, this conclusion to "The Game," quoted here in Alex Zucker's translation, serves well as an introduction to Blatný's work:

> To carry the world around,
> like the stone of Sisyphus, in my head,
> this was all I knew how to do and that is very little,
> just as in Chinese poetry
> there is sometimes very little,
> nothing more than the sky and a bird flying across it,
> a bird flying across it; a bird, but a real one,
> one that has ceased to play the game, one that will play no more,
> and for that little thing, a thing next to nothing
> I would put my leg on the block,
> just like the Passerby,
> just like the Passerby,
> only the other way round.

—Veronika Tuckerová, 2007

Blatný in English

Very little of Blatný's poetry has appeared in English translation to date. The intent of this volume, which presents selections culled from the full span of the poet's writing life, is not to be exhaustive, or even representative, but rather to provide an introduction to the poet's work for the English-speaking reader. Our selection, especially for the sections from *This Night* and *In Search of Present Time*, is indebted to the bilingual French-Czech volume of Blatný's poetry (*Le Passant*) that was published in Paris in 1992 and edited by Zbyněk Hejda. We are grateful to him for his support of this project. The remaining selections, from *Brno Elegies*, *Old Addresses*, and *Bixley Remedial School*, resulted from our own deliberations in conjunction with the will of the translators. A happy by-product of this approach is the diversity of translation styles and approaches represented in the book: This diversity seems appropriate given the range of styles found in the poet's own work. The challenges of translation—from questions of whether and how to reproduce rhyme and meter to the peculiar resistance of multilingual poems—become more apparent than usual in a collection of this sort, and in response we have asked each translator or team of translators to contribute a working note to the book (pp. 165-169). "About this edition" (p. 161) discloses our source texts and editing process, and gives a glimpse into the challenge of working with a poet whose publication history is complicated by particular historical, political, and logistical factors.

Finally, we are also including a short section of poems which Blatný wrote primarily in English, some of which have been published previously in Czech magazines, and some of which are published here for the first time. We would like to thank Antonín Petruželka for volunteering his significant editorial contributions to the last three sections of the book (*Old Addresses*, *Bixley Remedial School* and *Another Poetical Lesson*) and for providing us with transcripts of the manuscripts, along with their photocopies and scans. We are also grateful to him for sharing his knowledge about Blatný's life and work. When Blatný died in 1990 he left behind thousands of pages of writing, very little of which has been published to date; what we offer of them here is only a taste of more to come.

In addition to those mentioned above, many people assisted in the making of this book. We are especially grateful to Dr. Jan Šmarda for his generous cooperation during our work on this book and for providing access to Blatný's photographs and correspondence. Thanks are also due to Josef Škvorecký for sharing his experiences as a publisher of Blatný's exilic poems, and to Prague-based editor Jan Šulc. David Vaughan, whose BBC radio program on Blatný aired just as this book was going to print, was a source of valuable information and has our thanks. We are grateful to Světlana and Luboš Jelínek from the Art Gallery in Chrudim, who graciously allowed us to reproduce the "muchláž" by Jiří Kolář that appears on the cover, and to the Archives of the Museum of National Literature in Prague for providing scans of Blatný's manuscripts. We also thank Bartoloměj Petruželka for making the scans of Blatný's manuscript pages which we used during the preparation of this book. Valuable editorial assistance was provided by Adéla Gemrothová, Jenny Smith, Genya Turovskaya, and Helen Skiba. And we would like to thank Elizabeth Beaujour for her course on Bilingual Writers at the Graduate Center of the City University of New York, which is where the conversation about Blatný's multilingual poetry which eventually led to this book began.

Finally, we would like to express our appreciation to the translators—Matthew Sweney, Justin Quinn, and Alex Zucker—who have worked tirelessly on this book and have waited so patiently to see the fruits of their labors. In his translator's note, Justin Quinn writes of his "strong sense that Blatný comes home, as it were, in English." As editors and publishers of translations, our hope is that for everything lost between languages or texts, something equally interesting is gained.

Veronika Tuckerová, editor

Anna Moschovakis, editor, Eastern European Poets Series

Matvei Yankelevich, series editor, Eastern European Poets Series

The Drug of Art

from

BRNO ELEGIES (1941)

TRANSLATED BY JUSTIN QUINN

Zatímco krajina se chvěla v mokré kápi,
seděl jsi u stolu, vychladlý, prázdný, sám.
Nad černí deštníků, jež liják zkrápí… zkrápí…,
pomalu sunul čas hodiny k hodinám.

Daleko od lidí, daleko od cizoty
zbytečných hovorů a nudných veselí
hrál vítr nad městem a rozházel si noty,
démanty velkých krup. A římsy řinčely.

Před chvílí supěl vlak, tvůj vlak, kterým ses vracel
do staré krajiny z únavných marných cest,
a příval neklidu lodičky rozkymácel
a mžilo bez konce na kalný, chladný vjezd.

A mžilo bez konce na buben plynojemu,
na stěhovací vůz, na měkký šedý šál.
Přítel je kdesi tam… Stále se vracíš k němu
studeným prostorem, kde vítr kraloval.

Vysmýčil každý kout pro velké odcizení,
pro strašnou prázdnotu, pro úzkost, jež se chví,
jež hučí blíž a blíž a brzo vzkřikne: Není,
není už blízkosti a není přátelství.

Někdy jsi oslovil ty ostatní, ty cizí.
Jsou v jiných krajinách. Mlýn mele naprázdno.
Pod vlnou hladiny hluboko ve tmě mizí
neschůdné skalisko a hrbolaté dno.

V chaluhách jezera se mihne chápající
mlčení němých ryb a pluje tiše dál.
A voda zrcadlí hory a lesy spící
v šumotu havrana, jenž tudy odlétal.

Měděný strom jak blesk osvětlil náhle zemi,
vyšel jsem do deště omýt si zprahlé rty.
Tys jednou povídal: „Jsme němí, němí, němí.“
Tak tedy chvilku slyš mou Píseň němoty.“

WHILE RAIN WENT rippling out across the land,
you shivered at a table, blank and alone.
The downpour drummed on all that black outspanned
by umbrellas. The hours, the hours edged on.

Far from people, far from their strange ways,
their tedious good cheer and useless prattle,
the wind waltzed scattering hailstones and staves
above the city. And all the windows rattled.

A train wheezed in just now, your train. You're back
in the old country from traveling about.
The inrush left boats bobbing in its wake
and drizzle on the clouded station-mouth.

And drizzle… drizzle on the gasometer's drum,
on the moving van, on a soft grey scarf wound round.
A friend is there somewhere… You always come
again to him through cold space swept by wind.

It cleans out every corner and such fear,
such absence and estrangement in the end
come booming closer, closer. They howl: Not here.
No-one is close and no-one to call friend.

You sometimes turned to strangers. They now sleep
in other lands. The mill grinds with no intake.
The rubbled bed and rockface, sheer and steep,
fade in the darkness of the rippled lake.

Amidst its weeds, there is the grasp and flash
of speechless fishes' silence, which then goes.
And the water mirrors hills and woods awash
in murmurs of the overflying crows.

A copper tree sparked and the earth was lit,
I went to wash my lips with rain. And yes,
you once said: "We are mute, mute, mute"
So listen for a moment to my Song of Muteness.

PLÁŇ SE TI OTVÍRÁ, když míjíš dlouhou zeď
zelené zahrady, zeď mrtvých na Centrálce.
Buš do ní zoufale a čekej odpověď,
jen vyplašený pták… odlétá… mizí v dálce.

Jen vyplašený pták odlétá oblohou
(skotačil na hrobech a hvízdal v keřích smrti)
a smyčka lítosti se zadrhuje, škrtí,
sleduješ jeho let, olovo na nohou.

Sleduješ jeho let, jak lehounce tam pluje,
jak jízva na nebi se zvolna zaceluje
nad poli, lukami a kolébáním vod.
Ta rýha stříbrná… ta rýžka… nit… a bod…

THE PLAIN SPREADS out from you when you've gone by
the cemetery wall where greensward glistens.
Beat on it desperately and in reply
a startled bird flies off into the distance.

And startled through the sky he loops and pegs,
who danced on graves and sang the dead his jokes.
Regret draws tighter, tighter, till it chokes.
You watch his flight, lead clipped onto his leg.

You watch his flight, how he lightly wheels,
a wound upon the sky that slowly heals
above the meadows, cradled by a beck.
That silver furrow... groove... that thread... a speck.

Kdybys tu se mnou šel, viděl bys, co mám rád.
Kostelík, strouha, most, krajina obyčejná,
všední a překrásná jak šedí vrabci z hejna,
řeka, stín kaštanu, hojivá vůně, chlad.

Tak voda ze studny na chvíli smyje prach,
který sc usadil na rozpáleném čele
a padá na knihy, na dopis od přítele
a tiše pokrývá obrazy na stěnách.

To bylo v červenci, já jsem se navracel,
ty jsi stál u okna a kývals mi už z dálky,
právě se vzbudily vlaštovky-povídalky,
jiskřící kohouti a zámek plný skel.

Hřebínek oblohy se vznítil o hřeben
lesnatých pahorků, s kterými splýval hebce.
Slyšel jsem čistý křik nad dílnou zlatotepce,
snídal jsem jahody a máslo brukví. Den!

If you came with me, you'd see what I like.
A church, a bridge, a ditch—this countryside
so ordinary and beautiful beside
a river, the chestnut's fragrant shade, its look.

So water from the well clears off the dust
that settled on a face ruddy and tanned,
and falls on books, on a letter from a friend,
and covers paintings, quietly drapes a bust.

It was July and I was coming back.
You at the window, nodding from afar,
the swifts just risen like an airborne bazaar,
glittering roosters, the castle's glassy stack.

And near the earth the sky was set ablaze
by wooded hills, then darkened from the top.
I heard a cry above the goldsmith's shop.
For breakfast I had strawberries. Such days!

Nad lomem u lesa je holá cementárna.
Šel jsem si nahoru uříznout z šípků prut.
Město se ztrácelo a řeka odnikud
míjela pod kopcem, lhostejná, líná, marná.

Mohl jsem jenom psát, jak proniká mě Nic.
V ubohém korytě s ní odtékaly týdny.
Odjížděl černý vlak, drkotající, bídný,
deštivé úterý se lesklo z kolejnic.

Krajinou pronikal zlý mlhovitý chlad
a krása vstávala, z nicoty, slavně, zvolna.
Proudila něžná zář: Hle, činžák, dvory, kolna!
Krumpáče zvonily. Hleděl jsem na západ.

Potichu zaléval zčernalé zahrádky
i láhve od piva, řinčící dole z vozů,
město se valilo, slyšel jsem do lomozu
řvát strachem dobytek, jejž hnali na jatky.

Opilý hlučný zpěv se nesl od kantin,
stmělo se pode mnou, zaslech jsem čvachtat kroky.
Utichal třeskot skla a ochraptělé sloky,
z tunelů pod náspy se nořil stín a stín.

Pak všecko zmizelo do lesů u Brna,
kde bloudí vůně hub a máta peprná
a dým se rozplynul v pasekách nad Svitavou.

Krvavé slzičky jsou roztroušeny travou,
my ale půjdeme dál, dál až na konec.
Ne, není radosti. A trýzeň je. A přec.

ABOVE THE WOODED quarry are cement-works.
I went up there to cut a rose-hip wand.
The city faded and the river panned
beneath the hill, dragging its sluggish murk.

With nothing in me I could only write,
and weeks flowed off with it along its bed.
A black train trundled by and left a thread
of rails that glinted in the rainy light.

And everywhere this wicked cold progressed
though beauty rose and rose amazingly.
Its fluent glow: a building, yards, an alley!
Pickaxes rang out. I looked toward the west.

Sundown poured on blackened plots, on car
after clanging car, on bottle-glass immured
in the splayed city. In all that din I heard
the cows go wailing to the abattoir.

Loud songs rose from the drinking halls,
steps squelching by, the dark spread up the hill,
the clink of glass and hoarse refrains gone still,
and shadows crowded from the railway tunnels.

Then everything faded in the woods near Brno,
where the scents of mint and mushroom flow,
and smoke dispersed in clearings near the river.

Amidst the grasses, blood-red petals quiver.
But we push on, push on, which is our will.
No. No joy. And hurt by it. And still.

from

THIS NIGHT (1945)

TRANSLATED BY MATTHEW SWENEY

TENTO VEČER

Pozoroval jsem zrníčka a nitky,
opřel jsem nůž   Naslouchejte tramvajím,
rád bych promluvil, jak řeknu tento večer,
zaštěkání   Opět   Nořící se vzhůru,
svou velkou knihu, v které listuji,
šumot kroků   Hustý   Stále na jednom místě
Něžně jsem sfoukl popel   Bilo půl deváté
V stínítku lampy jsem slyšel   Anebo snad
Signály, křížící se jako stébla
Zhasl jsem   A zvenku zavanula

Tento večer   Jak řeknu tento večer
Teď například   A jak se jmenuje ten pavouček
Vstanu, beru si své staré zápisky
Rouaultův obraz   Myslím na
Kdy vás poznám, zdálo se mi o vás
Dnešek   Neustále vzniká na všech místech,
na tratích, v městech, v lesích, na frontách
Náhle   Zazvoní zdola   Trapná vzpomínka
Hmyz mezi řádky
S štíhlým, žlutě kroužkovaným trupem

Teď na malíčku   Jindy   Klopýtá po schůdcích
Temné prádelny   Po
Neslyším nic než bzukot
Také ovšem   Otevru dveře, pruh světla
Nikdo mi nenechal vzkaz…
Sešity   Slovník   Hleděl jsem na slaměnky
Bez hnutí   Jako v nich šustí měsíc
Hendrikje   Totiž   Vlak se rozjížděl
Sahal jsem po klice, co člověk vidí v jednom okamžiku
Všecky dny   Všecky noci   Právě v této chvíli
Zurčící z vodovodů   Hudby   Naslouchejte

1. 9. 1942

THIS NIGHT

I observed grains and threads,
I set the knife   Listen to the trams
I would like to speak, as I say this night,
barking   Again   Plunging upward,
my big book, which I leaf through,
the rustle of footsteps   Thick   Still on one spot
Gently I blew away ash   Eight-thirty struck
In the lampshade I heard   Or perhaps
Signals, crossing like stalks
I turned out the light   And outside it was gently blowing

This night   As I say this night
Now for example   And what is that little spider called
I get up, I take my old notes
Rouault's painting   I think about
When I will recognize you, I dreamed of you
This day   Arising unceasingly everywhere,
on the tracks, in cities, in the woods, on the fronts
Suddenly   Ringing from below   Embarrassing memory
Insect between the lines
With a thin, yellow-ringed abdomen

Now on my little finger   Some other time   Stumbling down the little stairs
Of a dark laundry room   After
I don't hear anything but buzzing
Also of course   I open the door, a beam of light
No one left me a note...
Notebooks   Dictionary   I gazed at the strawflowers
Motionless   How the moon rustles inside them
Hendrikje   That is to say   Train picked up speed
I reached for the handle, what can be seen in an instant
All days All nights Right at this moment
Gurgling from the water mains   Music   Listen

September 1, 1942

UDÁLOST

Všecky se právě někam chystaly.
Ptal jsem se Hedvičky, kam jedou.
Na pohřeb.
Prý hrozně nerada. V těch vyšlapaných botkách.

Nových by bylo škoda v tomto počasí.
Na viaduktu láteřily vlaky.
Nakonec všichni.
Hrozně neradi.

Tak se tam mějte dobře.
Všecky se usmály.
Švagrová čistila boty.
Pršelo. Nashledanou.

1942

EVENT

They were all just about to leave.
I asked Hedvička where they were going.
To the funeral.
She really doesn't want to. Not in those wornout shoes.

It would be a shame to wear new ones in this weather.
Trains grumble on the viaduct.
All of them, finally.
They really don't want to.

So have a good time there.
They all laughed.
Sister-in-law cleaned her shoes.
It rained. Bye-bye.

1942

MALÁ VARIACE

Čtvrtek dvacet hodin. Na stole:
Zápalky, cigarety, tabák, nůž a lampa.
Mé nástroje.
Už znáš mou hudbu z pěti, šesti věcí,
Už znáš mou hudbu z pěti, šesti věcí,
Můj malý zpěv.
Jak syčí na kamnech, jak bublá v tichu
Zpěv okamžiku,
Který je jenom jednou v dějinách.

Zápalky, cigarety, tabák, nůž a lampa.
A na všem leží prach.
Neslyšně klusající kůň jej nese na kopytu.
Prach vymřelého bytu.
Prach vymřelého bytu.
Naposled zvířený se ztrácí v dějinách.

Čtvrtek dvacet hodin. Na stole:
Noviny, cigarety, tabák, nůž a lampa.
Noviny: Papandreu, Pierlot.
Nábytek: Divan, kredenc s ornamenty.
Můj malý zpěv.
Liják sem šplíchá špatně zabedněným oknem.
I v bytě zmoknem!
I v bytě zmoknem!
A ještě horší prkna
Zbudou na rakev.

7. 12. 1944

SMALL VARIATION

Thursday 8 pm. On the table:
Matches, cigarettes, tobacco, knife, and lamp.
My tools.
You already know my music from five or six things,
You already know my music from five or six things,
My little song.
As it sizzles on the stove, as it bubbles in quietude
The song of the interlude,
Which happens only once in history.

Matches, cigarettes, tobacco, knife, and lamp.
And dust on all of them.
The silent horse gallops and carries it on hoof.
Dust of the barren flat.
Dust of the barren flat.
For the last time unsettled, is lost into history.

Thursday 8 pm. On the table:
Newspapers, cigarettes, tobacco, knife, and lamp.
Newspapers: *Papandreu, Pierlot.*
Furniture: Divan, ornamented credenza.
My little song.
Big drops hit the badly boarded window with a splat.
We'll get wet inside the flat!
We'll get wet inside the flat!
And even shabbier boards
Will be left for the coffin.

December 7, 1944

DRUHÁ

U železničního mostu
Smutná píseň je ve vzduchu.
V smetí tlí dopis: „Drahá Albertinko!"
Sobota večer. Kdepak asi je?
Kytice, křeslo, v kterém sedávali,
A staré věci toho pokoje.
Kytici vyhodili koncem léta
A křeslo, v kterém sedávala teta,
Se zvolna rozpadá.

U železničního mostu
Smutná píseň je ve vzduchu.
Jak čmouha poletuje tiše po obloze.
A je to píseň válečného města,
Píseň starostí,
Starostí, smrtí, lásky, žárlivosti.
Studený vítr prohrabává smetiště,
Haraší v plechovkách a hvízdá na kosti.

U železničního mostu
Smutná píseň je ve vzduchu.
(V barácích za tratí se rozsvěcují světla.)
Na chvíli utkví v žlutém oblaku.
Vyzáblá děvčátka jdou k předměstskému kinu,
Je slyšet maďarštinu
Špinavých vojáků.
Tu tmavou řeč, tu tmavou skřípající violu.

Stál tady cirkus? Byli to cirkusáci
Tam v polích za konečnou stanicí?
Nějaký ženský hlas se stále vrací

SECOND

De railroadbridge's
A sad song in de air.
                    Langston Hughes

Dear Albertine
                    Marcel Proust

The railroad bridge is
A sad song in the air.
A letter decomposes in the trash: "Dear Albertine"
Saturday night. Where has she been?
Bouquet, the chair in which they sat,
And the old things of this room.
They threw away the bouquet at the end of summer
And the chair in which auntie slumbered
Is falling apart on its own.

The railroad bridge is
A sad song in the air.
Like a smudge floating quietly in the sky.
A song of a war town it is,
A song of despair,
Death, love, jealousy, despair.
A cold wind rakes through the trash,
Scraping the tins and whistling through the bones and ash.

The railroad bridge is
A sad song in the air.
(Lights go on in the houses behind the tracks.)
In a little while it gets stuck in a yellow cloud.
On the outskirts, skinny girls go to the cinema
You can hear the Hungarian
Of dirty soldiers.
That dark speech, that dark scraping viola.

Did the circus stop here? Were the circus people there
In the fields behind the end of the line?
Some woman's voice keeps coming back

S havranem na kštici.
Ö,ö,ü,ü, ty temné samohlásky,
Temné a oblé jako kadeře.
Večere plný vší!
Vší, potu, lásky,
Strádání, klepajících na dveře!

Vidím je vcházet do cizího bytu,
Do bytu, kde jsem také kdysi psal.
Mrtví se scházejí a šelestí tu.
Kytice, křeslo, stuhy a tak dál.
Už znáš mou píseň z pěti, šesti věcí,
Můj malý zpěv?
(V smetí tlí dopis: Albertinko… Ty…)
Stále se opakuje jako životy.

3. 3. 1945

With a raven on a tuft of hair.
Ö, ö, ü, ü, those dark vowels,
Dark and rounded like curls.
Nights full of lice!
Lice, sweat, love,
Destitution, knocking on the door!

I see them go into a strange flat,
Into a flat where I too once wrote
The dead meet here and rustle about.
Bouquet, chair, ribbons, and more.
You already know my song from five or six things,
My little song?
(In the trash a letter rots: Albertine... You...)
It keeps repeating, like lives do.

March 3, 1945

TŘETÍ

Čekám na svoji mammy—
Je to smrt.
Otálí ještě kdesi na ulici,
Otálí před domem.
A věci na stole jsou jí už plny,
A věci na stole jsou jí už plny:
Papíry, knihy, džbán.
Čekám na svoji mammy—
Je to smrt.
Přichází potichu, sype se jako prášek,
Neviditelná zatím, ale tu.
Slyším ji přešlapovat dole v zbořeništích,
Zbylých tu od prvního náletu.

Neděle odpoledne. Zastřelují děla.
A proutím, ještě holým, fičí chlad.
Nějaká harmonika ohlašuje jaro,
Nějaká harmonika ohlašuje jaro
Přes chodby, přes dvory.
Kohout se trhá vzadu na obloze.
Čekám na svoji mammy—
Je to smrt.
Čtu z věcí na stole:
Papíry, knihy… Spánek.
Lítost jej přivolává. (Albertinko, Ty.)
Ale Evropa se dává na cesty.

4. 3. 1945

THIRD

Waiting for my mammy—
She is Death.
(…)
But the boys are setting off on their journey.
            Langston Hughes

Waiting for my mammy—
She is Death.
She is waiting around somewhere on the street,
Waiting around in front of the house.
And the things on the table are full of her already,
And the things on the table are full of her already:
Papers, books, a pitcher.
Waiting for my mammy—
She is Death.
She comes quietly, falling down like dust,
Invisible, but all the while here.
I hear her walking below in the ruins
The first air raid left there.

Sunday afternoon. The big guns start firing.
And cold whistles through the branches, still bare.
A concertina announces Spring,
A concertina announces Spring
Across the hallways, across the courtyards.
Fire on the horizon.
Waiting for my mammy—
She is Death.
I read from the things on the table:
Papers, books... Sleep.
Sorrow beckons it. (Albertine, You.)
But Europe is setting off on journeys too.

March 4, 1945

ČTVRTÁ

F. H.

Naprostá opuštěnost, hustý prach,
Ležela na trámech a na cihlách,
Naprostá opuštěnost, soumrak padal.
Naprostá opuštěnost, hustý prach,
Ležela na trámech a na cihlách,
Naprostá opuštěnost, soumrak padal,
Přes tváře namačkané v tramvajích,
Přelétal řídký rozmrzelý sníh,
Městem se rozléhala zase kanonáda.

Naprostá opuštěnost, hustý prach,
Ležela na stole a na knihách,
Naprostá opuštěnost, soumrak padal.
Naprostá opuštěnost, hustý prach.
Ležela na stole a na knihách,
Naprostá opuštěnost, soumrak padal.
V některém z domů, jako tolikrát,
Pomalý noční chodec vyšel z vrat
A sníh mu letěl přes rozrytá záda.

Psala tam válka, únava a strach,
Krčil se v trámoví a na cihlách,
Naprostá opuštěnost, soumrak padal.
Psala tam válka, únava a strach,
Krčil se v trámoví a na cihlách,
Naprostá opuštěnost, soumrak padal.
A tváře namačkané život na život
Sbíhaly se tam všecky v malý bod,
Zatímco městem zněla kanonáda.

11. 3. 1945

FOURTH

For F. H.

Absolute desolation, thick dust drops,
Upon the roof beams and housetops,
Absolute desolation, dusk has fallen.
Absolute desolation, thick dust drops,
Upon the roof beams and housetops,
Absolute desolation, dusk has fallen,
Across the faces pushed together on the trams,
Sullen snow flurries scatter and land
The town shook again from artillery flak.

Absolute desolation, thick dust drops,
Upon the books and tabletops,
Absolute desolation, dusk has fallen.
Absolute desolation, thick dust drops,
Upon the books and tabletops,
Absolute desolation, dusk has fallen.
In one of the houses, as so often before,
The slow night walker emerged from the door
And snow flew across his furrowed back.

War was written there, fatigue and fear,
Cringing in the roof beams and veneer,
Absolute desolation, dusk has fallen.
War was written there, fatigue and fear,
Cringing in the roof beams and veneer,
Absolute desolation, dusk has fallen.
And faces pushed together, life against life
Converging together on the point of a knife,
While the town still rang with artillery flak.

March 11, 1945

PÁTÁ

Kdepak jsi asi teď, teď právě v tuto chvíli,
V ten přesný okamžik, dnes, kdy jsem začal psát.
Je to ta známá pustá neděle,
Je to ta známá pustá neděle,
Ten dobře známý táhlý zpívající hlas.
Zoufale monotonně znovu, znovu, znovu,
Zoufal monotonně znovu, znovu, znovu,
A zas a zas.
Nějaká zaklínací formule
Přelétla pavlač: Merde!
V hlubokém tichu vážně odpovídá
Das deutsche Volkskonzert.

Kdepak jsi asi teď, teď právě v tuto chvíli,
V ten přesný okamžik, kdy tuto báseň čteš.
Bylo už po válce? Byl podzim? Bylo jaro?
Kdosi mě doprovázel venku na kytaru
A já jsem hrál.
Byla ta známá pustá neděle,
Byla ta známá pustá neděle,
Kytice, křeslo, stuhy a tak dál.
Váš byt byl prázdný: Odešla za milencem.
Nějaký černě ustrojený pán se táhl s věncem.
Byla ta známá pustá neděle.

Vzpomeň si, Albertinko, potom na ty dny,
Bělásek zelný ležel na podlaze,
Kopali zákopy, bombardovali v Praze,
Bělásek zelný, zimou zemdlený.
Měl jste ho zabít, řekla Františka,
Naklade vajíček, to zas bude škody!
Vzpomeň si, Albertinko, na ty dny!
Das deutsche Volkskonzert se táhl kamsi s věncem.
Ten dobře známý táhlý zpívající hlas.
Zoufale monotonně znovu, znovu, znovu,
Zoufale monotonně znovu, znovu, znovu
A zas a zas.

1945

FIFTH

I wonder where you are, right this instant,
In this very moment, today, when I have begun to write.
It is that famous empty Sunday,
It is that famous empty Sunday,
That famous singing voice and its wailing refrain.
Desperately monotonous over, and over, and over,
Desperately monotonous over, and over, and over,
And again and again.
Some magic rite
Flew over the balcony: Merde!
Gravely answering in the deep silence
Das deutsche Volkskonzert.

I wonder where you are, right this instant,
In this very moment, when you read this poem.
Was it after the war already? Was it Autumn? Was it Spring?
Someone accompanied me outside on guitar
And I strummed upon the strings.
It was that famous empty Sunday,
It was that famous empty Sunday,
Bouquet, chair, ribbons, and more.
Your flat was empty: She's taken a lover's leave.
Some gentleman in black struggled with a wreath.
It was that famous empty Sunday.

Remember, Albertine, later, those days,
A Large White butterfly was lying on the floor,
They dug trenches, bombarded Prague some more,
A Large White butterfly, weary of winter's ways.
You should have killed it, Františka says,
It will do harm with the eggs it lays!
Remember, Albertine, those days!
Das deutsche Volkskonzert struggled somewhere with a wreath.
That famed singing voice and its wailing refrain.
Desperately monotonous over, and over, and over,
Desperately monotonous over, and over, and over
And again and again.

1945

from

IN SEARCH OF PRESENT TIME (1947)

TRANSLATED BY MATTHEW SWENEY

MÍSTA

Místa, která jsme opustili, žijí dál.
Kůň kluše, dítě křičí, matka otvírá dveře:
„Tady to není, tady to není, tak nevím, kam to přišlo." Hledají.
Hledají něco, pobíhají po bytě.
Hledají místa, která jsme opustili, hledají místa, kde jsme kdysi byli.
Spěchají k nádraží a pomyslí si: Dům.
Dům zůstal.
Kam odjíždějí?
Na pohřeb sestry. Navždy. Za synem.
Stařenka zůstává. Stařenku neberou s sebou.
Nechají doma hvízdat Meluzínu.
Hodiny neberou s sebou.
Hodiny bijí v prázdném pokoji.

PLACES

The places we've abandoned live on.
The horse is trotting, the child is screaming, mother is opening the door:
"It's not here, it's not here, I don't know where it went." They're looking.
They're looking for something, running around the flat.
Looking for the places we've abandoned, looking for the places where we used to be.
They're hurrying to the train station, thinking: The house.
The house has remained.
Where are they traveling?
To sister's burial. Leaving for good. To the son's.
The old woman remains. They don't take her with them.
They're leaving Melusina home to whistle.
Taking no clock with them.
The clock chimes in an empty room.

HISTORICKÝ OBRAZ

Zatímco děti pouštěly své lodičky
Vítr foukal tak prudce že kapky vodotrysku
Postříkaly občas
Nějakého chodce i velmi vzdáleného
Zatímco děti chytaly své lodičky
Pan Uang Ši Šieh
Přenechal řízení schůze panu Bidaultovi
Bylo slyšet jak zurčí voda šesti prameny
Chrličů z listnatých ozdob
Delacroixovy fontány a bylo slyšet
Jak padá kousek kůry z platanu
Na hladinu nádrže mezi pírka větvičky a smetí.

Pan Bidault pravil: Mírová konference je skončena.

HISTORICAL PAINTING

While the children were playing with their little sailboats
The wind blew so hard that droplets from the fountain
Sometimes splashed
Onto a pedestrian even some distance away
While the children were catching their little sailboats
Mr. Wang Shi Shieh
Turned the meeting over to Mr. Bidault
The whoosh of the water could be heard from the six jets
Of the spouts carved with leaves
In Delacroix's fountain, and you could hear
How a little bark falls from the sycamore
Onto the surface of the reservoir amidst feathers, branches, pond scum.

Mr. Bidault said: The Peace Conference is over.

ZPĚV

Tisíce kilometrů ode mne,
podobna lesům, zvěři a řekám a oboře
v krajině mého dětství s dřevěným letohrádkem,
kde netopýři se právě probouzejí v trámoví.
Tisíce kilometrů ode mne.
Tisíce kilometrů ode mne, a přece neustále přítomná,
tak jako mrtví v starých bytech, které zahlédneme pod lampou, číst, klidně číst
       slepnoucím okem
v nějaké knize rukou psaných receptů,
13 dkg másla, 4 žloutky, 30 d. cukru,
anebo listovat v obrázkovém časopise z roku 1928 s pohledy z přístavů
se sudy, povalujícími se mezi lodicemi
nad hustou špinavou vodou plnou drtin
a kusů dřeva pod okrajem nábřeží
(malý orchestr na nároží prodává populární písně),
s fotografiemi černošských plastik, hvězd music-hallů, tanečnic, tahitských domorodců,
       jazzových zpěváků, Rodinových soch, moderních koupelen,
a mužů v buřinkách, kteří spravují dlažbu roku
1900,
zatímco jiní, v cylindrech, nastupují zvolna
na střechu koňské dráhy s nápisem GARE de L'EST.

Nedávno jsem se tam ještě procházel kolem železné mříže,
pod níž se prostírají nástupiště a haly, kam jsme přijeli,
odkud jsme sestoupili do metra,
odkud jsme vystoupili potom na stanici
La Motte-Picquet-Grenelle,
byli jsme v Paříži,
Eiffelka byla na dosah ruky jako nějaký model,
jako nějaký model Eiffelky postavený
na psací stůl,
děti bruslily na kolečkových bruslích
na plošině mezi dvěma schodišti,
jimiž se ze dvou stran
přichází k Trocadéru,

SONG

Thousands of kilometers away from me,
similar to the woods, wildlife, rivers and park
in the landscape of my childhood, with a wooden gazebo,
where bats actually stir in the eaves.
Thousands of kilometers away from me.
Thousands of kilometers away from me, and yet still near,
just like the dead in old flats, whom under the lamp we see straining to read, read in peace
         with a failing eye
in a book of hand-written recipes,
130 grams of butter, 4 egg yolks, 300 grams of sugar
or else turn the pages of an illustrated magazine from 1928 with pictures of harbors
with barrels scattered between ships
atop the thick dirty water full of sawdust
and wood scraps below the shore's edge
(a small orchestra on the corner sells popular songs),
with photographs of African carvings, music-hall stars, dancers, Tahitian natives, jazz singers,
         Rodin's statues, modern bathrooms,
and men in bowlers fixing the pavement in
1900,
meanwhile others, in top hats, casually take their seats
on the roof of a horse-drawn tram marked GARE de L'EST.

Not long ago I was there, walking past the iron railings
under which extend the platforms and the halls where we arrived,
from there we descended into the Metro
from there we descended at the station
La Motte-Picquet-Grenelle,
we were in Paris,
you could reach out and touch the Eiffel Tower as if it were a model,
like some model of the Eiffel Tower placed
upon a writing table,
children skated on rollerskates
on the platform between two stairways,
which on both sides
lead to Trocadéro,

později jsem tam často chodíval
s psem Youki
pod vznešenou klenbou čtyřřadých alejí,
kaštany padaly prudce a plnými hrstmi,
list, list, list, list,
přicházel podzim,
přicházel podzim, přicházel podzim, přicházel podzim,
koleje zasypány vzpomínaly na tramvaj.

Tisíce kilometrů ode mne, na místech, o nichž nevím.
A která neví o mně, tisíce kilometrů ode mne.
Tisíce kilometrů ode mne.
Tisíce kilometrů ode mne, v krajině mého dětství.
S ropuchou v měsíčním paloučku, pozorující jezdkyni,
která pak mizí, která pak ubíhá tryskem,
alejí stoupají k zámku podél obory.
Tisíce kilometrů ode mne.
Tisíce kilometrů ode mne kolem křižování plotu, kterým je vidět labutě s hadovitými krky.
Tisíce kilometrů ode mne.
Tisíce kilometrů ode mne kolem zámecké sýpky,
kolem slepého domu s okny zarůstajícími pavučinami, kolem hospodářských stavení.
Tisíce kilometrů ode mne na malém pahorku, který se jmenuje Křišťálov,
tam, kde modrozelené mouchy, veliké jako třpytící se knoflíky, obletují zmačkané papíry se
        zbytky jídel a lejna výletníků,
tam, kde noc všecko zatápí a proměňuje, tam, kde měsíc
naplňuje svá tichá akvária
hnojišť a dvorů, dlážděných kočičími hlavami,
tam, kde je svět a vesmír mimo mne a ve mně a všude a jinde než všude,
tisíce kilometrů ode mne.

I often walked there later
with Youki the dog
beneath the heavenly bowers of the four-laned avenues,
chestnuts fell sharply and in fistfuls,
leaves, leaves, leaves, leaves,
Autumn came,
Autumn came, Autumn came, Autumn came,
the smothered tracks remembered the tram.

Thousands of kilometers away from me, in places I don't know.
And which don't know me, thousands of kilometers away from me.
Thousands of kilometers away from me.
Thousands of kilometers away from me, in the landscape of my childhood.
With a toad in a moon glade, watching the horsewoman,
who then disappears, who then gallops by,
along leafy lanes ascending past the gardens to the chateau.
Thousands of kilometers away from me.
Thousands of kilometers away from me along the slatted fence through which can be
        glimpsed snake-necked swans.
Thousands of kilometers away from me.
Thousands of kilometers away from me, around the chateau granary,
around the blinded house growing cobwebs in its windows, around the farm buildings.
Thousands of kilometers away from me, on a small hill named Křišťálov,
where bluegreen flies big as glistening buttons buzz over crumpled paper, crumbs, and
        picnickers' crap,
there, where the night floods and changes everything, there, where the moon
fills its quiet aquariums
of dungheaps and courtyards paved with cobblestones,
there, where the world and universe is outside me and inside me, and everywhere and
        elsewhere than everywhere,
thousands of kilometres away from me.

DRUHÝ

Docela blízko u mne, zde v tomto pokoji
strýček Josef se učí esperanto a brnká na kytaru,
jen malý kousek odtud, docela blízko u mne, ve čtvrtém rozměru,
docela blízko u mne a jednou nohou,
a jednou nohou skoro ve třetím,
docela blízko u mne šeptá: Mi estas esperantisto! Parolu esperante, Ivano!
Jste všichni v tomto bytě.
Docela blízko u mne mrtvý roznašeč z půjčovny obrázkových časopisů otvírá právě dveře.
Docela blízko u mne babička bere obrázkový časopis.
Bylo to první den. Právě se předplatila. Docela blízko u mne.
Jste všichni v tomto bytě.
Mrtvý hudební skladatel, kterého milovala, se usmívá z černého rámečku.
Docela blízko u mne smrt neustále přítomná kosí hudební skladatele.
Docela blízko u mne esperantisté odcházejí v davech do záhrobí.
Jste všichni v tomto bytě.
Strýček Josef se brání: Mi estas esperantisto!
Docela blízko u mne smrt ukazuje tiše na dveře.
A strýček Josef odchází váhavě do jídelny, docela blízko u mne.
Docela blízko u mne sestupuje po schodech.
Jste všichni v tomto bytě.
Prosím vás, dejte už jednou spravit tu starou singrovku!
Zašeptá někdo kdesi docela blízko u mne.
Docela blízko u mne,
jste všichni v tomto bytě.
Byla to sice kruhovka, ale staršího typu.
Jsme všichni v tomto bytě.
Jen strýček Josef právě vyšel do dvora.

SECOND

Quite close to me, here in this room
Uncle Josef is learning Esperanto and strumming on his guitar,
just a little ways away from here, quite close to me, in the fourth dimension,
quite close to me and with one foot,
and with one foot almost in the third,
quite close to me he whispers: Mi estas esperantisto! Parolu esperante, Ivano!
You are all in this apartment.
Quite close to me a dead delivery boy from the lending library just opened the door.
Quite close to me grandma takes the picture pages.
It was the first day. She had just subscribed. Quite close to me.
You are all in this apartment.
The dead composer, whom she loved, smiles from his black frame.
Quite close to me Death, ever present, reaps the composers.
Quite close to me the Esperantists are leaving en masse to the hereafter.
You are all in this apartment.
Uncle Josef answers back: Mi estas esperantisto!
Quite close to me Death quietly points to the door.
And Uncle Josef goes out grudgingly to the dining room, quite close to me.
Quite close to me he descends the stairs.
You are all in this apartment.
Would you please finally fix that old Singer!
Someone somewhere quite close to me whispers.
Quite close to me,
you are all in this apartment.
It was a circular Singer, but an older model.
We are all in this apartment.
But Uncle Josef has just entered the courtyard.

TERRESTRIS

Každý večer,
o desíti, o jedenácti,
někdy později,
nájemník z prvního poschodí vychází z domu a zamyká,
bublání klíče stoupá
tmavou nádrží,
pak slyším jeho kroky,
jeho každodenní noční procházku
kolem bloku domů, ohraničeného čtyřmi ulicemi.

Na jedné z nich
nájemník z prvního poschodí se chvilku zastavuje
na silnici před průčelím rožáku,
zatímco nad střechami se zdraví
sny,
spěchající právě křížem krážem
k ložím svých spáčů a smekající na pozdrav,
hluboko smekající
komíny, hvězdy, korouhvičky dýmů.

A ještě výše než sny,
mezi věžemi anebo návršími
toho kterého města, mezi pahorky
zaniklých vinic
anebo vinohradů v plném rozkvětu,
na svazích, kterými se schází přímo k moři,
zjevuje se
někdy
čarodějnice Terrestris.

Chodec ji potom vidí, jak prochází
mezi sromy a sloupy a ploty a anténami,
tu a tam zmizí její štíhlá vysoká postava,
její hrb,
její kulhající chromá noha, její berla,

TERRESTRIS

Every evening,
around ten, around eleven,
sometimes later,
the tenant from the first floor leaves the house and locks up,
the bubbling of the keys rises
through the dark reservoir,
then I hear his footsteps,
his daily evening stroll
around the block of houses lined by four streets.

On one of these
the first floor tenant stops for a minute
on the street beside the façade of the corner house,
while above the rooftops, dreams
greet one another,
and speed criss-cross
to the bedrooms of their dreamers, tipping their hats,
bowing deeply
chimneys, stars, weathervanes of smoke.

And even higher than dreams,
among the towers and hills
of some town, among the slopes
of vanished vineyards
and vineyards in full bloom,
on the slopes which go all the way to the sea,
appears
sometimes
the witch Terrestris.

The walker then sees her, how she walks
between trees and columns and fences and antennas,
here and there her slim tall figure disappears,
her hump,
her hobbling club foot, her crutches,

aby se za okamžik zase vynořila,
chodec ji vidí klečet nad průzračnou studánkou,
hladina zrcadlí její oči a její oči
zrcadlí chvějicí se hladinu.

Chodec ji potom vidí, jak se sklání
nad malým ptákem vypadlým z hnízda a jak jej zahřívá,
jak se pak zase zvedá a jak jej na odchodu
trošičku něžně ještě přišlápne,
jen co by zapraskaly tiše jeho křehké kosti a
jen co by drobné srdce zcela nedotlouklo,
chodec ji potom vidí,
jak zvolna odchází,
mírná a laskavá matka všeho živoucího.

Jak měsíc neustále svítí na její útlé hrdlo,
ačkoli mlčí, plné melodie,
její kreténské vole průsvitní
jak bříško baňaté láhve, za jehož sklem
lze spatřit ráje ptáčků mezi květinami—
jsou to červení a žlutí kolibříci, sající nektar v letu
za sotva znatelného kolébání
velikých kalichů.

Zděšení pozemšťané marně zahánějí toto zjevení
znamením kříže, moudrými průpovídkami
uklidňujících náboženských obřadů,
marně se dotýkají
tajemných ochraňujících
kořenů srágory
v podobě různých malých
bezmocných trpaslíků,
bezmocných proti majestátu velké Terrestris.

Tisíce, milióny mladíků
sní
o krásné Terrestris,

how in an instant she pops back up,
the walker sees her kneel by the clear well
the surface reflecting her eyes and her eyes
reflecting the quivering surface.

The walker then sees her, how she leans
over a small bird fallen from the nest and how she warms it,
how she then arises and how on leaving
she steps on it a bit gently,
just so as to quietly break its delicate bones and
just so that its little heart will not entirely stop beating,
the walker then sees her,
how slowly she leaves,
the meek and mild mother of all the living.

How the moon ever shines on her slender throat,
though silent, full of melody,
her cretinous craw diaphanous
as a bulbous bottle's belly; behind its glass
a paradise of birds can be glimpsed among the flowers—
there are red and yellow hummingbirds, sipping nectar in flight
meanwhile the barely visible rocking
of giant goblets.

The terrified earth dwellers exorcise this apparition in vain
via the sign of the Cross, the sage adages
of soothing religious ceremonies,
vainly touching upon
the dark salvational
manduck roots
in the form of sundry small
powerless dwarves,
powerless against the majesty of the great Terrestris.

Thousands, millions of youths
dream
of the beautiful Terrestris,

tisíce, milióny
mladíků
sní
o daleké sladké zemi Koprofagů,
o plodu zapomnění
na všecko kromě tebe, Terrestris.

Za město
do Háje zamilovaných, do Háje vzdechů
kladou si ve snu tuto zázračnou krajinu,
za město do Čubčího háje,
kde kočky a můry létají haluzemi, kde
plstnatá dlouhozobka
třepotá křídly, sosáček v trubkovitém květu, kde
včely snášející maz ušní se slétnou
tu a tam ke kadeřím úlů krásné Terrestris.

Tisíce, milióny mladíků
padají obličejem
do těchto hustých vlnících se vlasů,
do těchto tuhých drsných vlasů, které se podobají
chuchvalcům žíní, čouhajících ze starých matrací,
tisíckrát pomočených
nesčetnou řadou mrtvých,
nesčetnou řadou mrtvých, kteří tu umírali,
kteří tu umírali, krásná Terrestris!

Tisíce, milióny mladíků tě vidí, Venuše Terrestris,
jak vystupuješ z pěnící se lázně,
čistá, odvšivená, plná blech,
tisíce, milióny milenců se procházejí
tvým jarním hájem, kde se otvírají žumpy
kvetoucích šeříků,
je slyšet vydechnuté věty letící nad krajinou:
Hle, bude pršet, záchody páchnou, podotkne kdosi a oni:
Ano, máme dnes vskutku hezké počasí.

thousands, millions
of youths
dream
of the faraway sweet land of the Coprophags,
of the fruit of forgetting
everything except you, Terrestris.

Behind the town
to the Grove of Those-in-Love, to the Grove of Sighs
where in their dreams they set this miraculous landscape,
behind the town to Bitch's Grove,
where kittens and moths fly through the boughs, where
a hummingbird hawk moth
flaps its felt wings, proboscis inside a flower's flute, where
bees carrying earwax fly down
hither and thither into the curly hives of beautiful Terrestris.

Thousands, millions of youths
falling face first
into those thick wavy curls,
into those dull rough hairs, which resemble
matted horsehair sticking up out of old mattresses,
a thousand times pissed on
by the countless ranks of the dead,
by the countless ranks of the dead, who died there,
who died there, beautiful Terrestris!

Thousands, millions of youths see you, Venus Terrestris,
how you arise from the foaming spa,
clean, deloused, full of fleas,
thousands, millions of lovers stroll
through your spring grove, where septic fields of
flowering lilacs are opening,
you can hear the sighing sentences flying over the terrain:
Ah, the outhouses stink, it's going to rain, remarks whoever and they:
Yes, we're certainly having nice weather today.

Tisíce, milióny mladíků
milují stromy
v tomto tvém jarním lese, krásná Terrestris,
milión opojených mladíků
se dává líbat
drsným jazykem kůr, posetým bradavkami,
tisíce, milióny mladíků
bez hnutí naslouchají
tlukotu v cévkách rašícího listí.

Tisíce, milióny mladíků
se drápe na tvé stromy,
milión opojených mladíků
se válí korunami.
„Pohleďte, jak jsou směšní!" povídá někdo, ale ty,
ty se jim neposmíváš, Terrestris.
Ó ty je miluješ, krásná čarodějnice, ó ty jim říkáš:
Ke mně, miláčkové, ke mně, spalte se, holoubkové,
shořte tak trošku všichni na popel!

Ach, jak ten Hlupák nerozuměl tvé písni, Terrestris,
ach, jak ten Hlupák neporozuměl našemu zpěvu!
Hle, jak jsou vznešení, voláš na něho, hle, jak jsou vznešení!
Hle, jak jsou vznešení, když lámou s praskotem větve!
S čenichem ponořeným do vlhkého lýka na lomu!
A s ústy šeptajícími slova lásky: Strome!
Miláčku strome, zvíře, hornino!
Miláčku vzduchu, vodo, miláčku slunce!
Miláčku smrti, miláčku narození!

Naslouchej této písni, ó Blbče, a ptej se, kdože ji zpívá!
Zpívá ji Duše? Zpívá ji Tělo? Odpověz!
To ty jsi vymyslel tuto obludnou dualitu?
Tvá zdechlá milenka Caelia tě opouští,
tvá zdechlá milenka Caelia tě zrazuje na každém kroku, ó Blbče!
Jednoho dne se to dovíš a budeš plakat,
jednoho dne se to dovíš a budeš naříkat:

Thousands, millions of youths
love the trees
there in your spring woods, beautiful Terrestris,
a million bedazzled youths
allow themselves to be kissed
by the rough tongue of bark, spangled with nipples,
thousands, millions of youths
stand still and listen
to the sound beating in the veins of the sprouting leaves.

Thousands, millions of youths
scramble up your trees,
a million bedazzled youths
lolling about in the treetops.
"Look how ridiculous they are!" someone says, but you,
you don't laugh at them, Terrestris.
O you love them, beautiful witch, O you tell them:
Come to me, lovers, to me, burn, my doves,
burn a little, to ashes, all of you!

O, how that Fool misunderstood your song, Terrestris,
O how that Fool didn't recognise our song!
Behold how gentle they are, you call to him, behold, how gentle they are!
Behold how gentle they are, when they break branches with a snap!
With snout sunk into the moist under bark!
And with mouth whispering words of love: Tree!
My lover tree, beast, rock!
My lover air, water, sun!
Lover death, lover birth!

Listen to this song, O Idiot, and ask, who's singing it?!
Is Spirit singing it? Is Body singing? Answer!
Was it you who invented this hideous duality?
Your dead lover Caelia leaves you,
your dead lover Caelia betrays you at every step, O Idiot!
One day you'll know and you will cry,
One day you'll know and you will cry:

Nebe je prázdné, prázdné, prázdné, prázdné, prázdné!
A tvoje mrzácká duše odpoví: Pustý svět.

Pak přijdeš za mnou a budeš prosit: Vrať mi mé podušky!
Vrať mi mé ohřáté pokličky na churavé břicho!
Vrať mi mé modlitbičky, vrať mi mé klystýry!
Navrať mi mého Anděla strážného! Budeš prosit
a já ti ukážu nebe, na němž se zjevuje
někdy
čarodějnice Terrestris,
anděl strašný, anděl bez odpovědi,
anděl otázek.

Budeš se bát, ó Blbče, budeš skučet:
Pryč s tímto strašidlem (budeš ji považovat za přelud),
jak onen proktofantasmista, který si posázel zadek pijavkami,
budeš si rychle shánět
nové pijavky,
nebudu se ti smát, ó příteli Blbče, i já se chvěji,
nebudu se ti smát, můj milý příteli!
Naslouchej ale dobře,
naslouchej ale dobře. Terrestris…

Zdá se, že otvírá ústa ten tichý obličej,
záhadný, mlčenlivý, ozářený lunou,
jako by chtěla něco říci, jako by…
jako by chtěla… Ticho! Ticho! Blbče!
Ačkoliv jenom otvírá ústa, rozumím!
Ano, jsem hluchoněmý!
Ó Blbče, můj drahý příteli, ó Blbče, můj bratře, slyš!
Mi-luj-mě!, říká Terrestris, rozuměl jsem jí dobře!
Žádá mě, abych ji miloval! Žádá mě, abych ji miloval!

Je to tvá jediná odpověď! křičím na ni,
je to tvá jediná odpověď, krásná Terrestris?!
Ale ona už mizí, ona se ztrácí,
ona se rozplývá

Heaven is empty, empty, empty, empty, empty!
And your crippled soul will answer: Barren world.

Then you'll come to me and you'll beg: Give me back my pillows!
Give me back my warm pot lids for my ailing belly!
Give me back my prayers, give me back my enemas!
Give me back my Guardian Angel! You'll beg
and I'll show you heaven, in which sometimes
appears
the witch Terrestris,
harridan angel, angel without answers,
angel of questions.

You'll be afraid, O Idiot, you'll wail:
Get this ghost away (you'll think it a mirage),
like the proctophantasmatist, who stuck leeches on his ass
you will quickly gather
new leeches,
I will not laugh at you, O Idiot friend, even I tremble,
I will not laugh at you, my dear friend!
Listen good,
listen good. Terrestris…

It looks as though that quiet face is opening its mouth,
mysterious, silent, moon-lit,
as if she wanted to say something, as if…
as if she wanted … Quiet! Shut up! Idiot!
Although she only mouths the words, I understand!
Yes, I am deaf and dumb!
O Idiot, my good friend, O Idiot, my brother, listen!
Love-me! says Terrestris, I understood her well!
She's asking me to love her! She's asking me to love her!

That's your only answer! I'm yelling at her,
is that your only answer, beautiful Terrestris?!
But she is already disappearing, she is vanishing
she's fading away,

v nějaký slabý,
měsíčný
obláček na obloze,
ještě v něm rozeznávám její vysokou postavu,
její kulhající nohu, její hrb…

Cítím tě ale, krásná Terrestris!
Jsi blízko!
Pod tímto otevřeným oknem ťukají tvoje podpatky!
Tvoje protéza, tvoje dřevěná noha kráčí po chodníku!
Cítím tě, slyším… její… klap-klap-klap…!
(tak jako kdysi v Paní Bovaryové),
a slepý žebrák zpívající svou píseň pod okny
na znamení, že báseň
se chýlí ke konci…

Možná, že tohoto večera
jdeš ke mně
naposled,
s vojáky, spěchajícími zpátky do kasáren,
s opilcem, hadrem, vránou v kostech zbořenisk,
s mladíky, kteří se vracejí z Háje zamilovaných
se zkrvaveným rtem, s vyraženými zuby,
nakaženi larvami mnišek a lykožroutů
a s chutí listí ještě na dně papil!

Možná, že tohoto večera jdeš ke mně naposled!
Blížíš se, stoupáš po schodech, otvíráš dveře
staré předsíně,
jdeš kolem trumeau, jdeš kolem „veliké garderoby“,
otvíráš pomalu dveře
mého pokoje,
stůj! zadrž, Terrestris! poslouchej! chci ti říci
nápěv svých písní, všech písní zpívaných pro tebe!
stůj! zadrž, Terrestris! poslouchej! chvilku, chvilku!

Otvírám jenom ústa, nevydávám hlas,
rozumíš dobře, co říkám, jsi hluchoněmá?!

into some weak,
moon-
cloud in the sky,
in which I can still make out her tall figure,
her club foot, her hump…

I can feel you, beautiful Terrestris!
You are close!
Your heels clip clop below this open window!
Your prosthesis, your wooden foot hobbling along the walk!
I feel you, I hear … her … clip-clap-club…!
(like once in Madame Bovary),
and the blind beggar singing his song under the windows
a sign the poem
is nearing its end…

Perhaps, this night
you are coming to me
for the last time,
with soldiers speeding back to the barracks,
with a drunk, a rag, a crow in the bones of ruins,
with youths returning from the Grove of Those-In-Love
with bloody lips, with smashed teeth,
infected by the larvae of Gypsy moths and bark beetles
with the taste of leaves in the taste buds!

Perhaps you're coming to me this night for the last time!
You're nearing, ascending the stairs, opening the doors
of the ancient foyer,
you walk around the trumeau, you walk around the "Grande garde-robe,"
you slowly open the door
to my room,
halt! stay there, Terrestris! listen! I want to tell you
the melody of my songs, all the songs sung for you!
halt! stay there, Terrestris! listen! a little while, just a little while!

I'm only opening my mouth, not giving voice,
do you understand well what I'm saying, are you a deaf-mute?!

můj nápěv: Přijímám tě, krásná Terrestris!
můj nápěv: Chci tě tak!
můj nápěv: Miluji tě, můj nápěv: Miluji tě!
ještě než přitiskneš ruce na mé hrdlo, Terrestris,
ještě než odložíš můj kabát do Velké garderoby…
netiskni ještě tolik! netiskni ještě tolik!
jen co by nedotlouklo…

Prosím tě, chtěl bych ještě
popadnout dech!
jedinkrát lapnout
ještě po dechu,
abych ti mohl… ještě naposled…
Mi… Mi-lu-ji tě,
krás-
ná
Te…

my song: I accept you, beautiful Terrestris!
my song: I want you so!
my song: I love you, my song: I love you!
even before you press your hands to my throat, Terrestris,
even before you place my coat in the Grande garde-robe…
don't press so hard! don't press so hard!
just so it won't entirely stop beating…

Please, I'd like
to catch my breath again!
just once to catch
my breath again
so I could … again for the last time…
I … I … love … you,
beau-ti-
ful
Te …

"THE GAME" (1947)

TRANSLATED BY ALEX ZUCKER

Když se Kolemjdoucí ráno probudil,
ranní můra
vstávala s ním
a spustila svůj malý motorek,
svůj malý ventilátor,
jenž vhání do dne zbytky uplynulé noci,
takzvané Nachtreste,
zvuk, jak by rozšlapával někdo pivní trubky,
ranní můra opustila lucernu,
svítilnu zavěšenou na mříž mezi hroty,
jiný si čistil rozežrané zuby zábradlí.

V některé z dalších koupelen pak třetí kloktal
strojním olejem,
zatímco Kolemjdoucí vycházel už z domu
a ranní můra s ním,
přivolávajíc různé bájeslovné bytosti,
například skřítky, Malé nepřátele,
z nichž jeden ihned hbitě přiskočil
a dával chodcům brky jako na fotbalu,
a vůbec fotbal,
a vůbec fotbal
byl rozšířený sport.

Teprve v poledne se trošku vyjasnilo,
skřítkové zalezli,
rádio vysílalo zemědělský rozhlas,
noviny přinášely zprávy o válce,
o příští válce, přesto všecko spalo,
oběd byl v žaludcích
a také Kolemjdoucí
si chvilku zdříml,
si chvilku zdříml
a měl tento sen:

Zdálo se mu, že jede s matkou, se svou patnáct let mrtvou matkou na vozíku pro mrzáky na dalekou cestu za takzvanou Oponu. Kolemjdoucí seděl vpředu a řídil, matka

WHEN THE PASSERBY awoke in the morning,
his morningmare
arose with him
and started up its little engine,
its little fan
that drives forth into the day the remainders of the previous night,
otherwise known as the *Nachtreste*,
making a sound like someone trampling beer lines,
the morningmare fluttered out of the lantern,
the lamp hung between the spiked points of a grill fence,
while someone else brushed his rotting railing's teeth.

In one of the next bathrooms down, a third gargled
with motor oil,
while the Passerby left the building
and his morningmare along with him,
summoning forth various mythical beings,
such as the Little Enemy hobgoblins,
one of whom nimbly leapt right in
and proceeded to trip pedestrians up, the way they do in soccer,
and for that matter soccer,
and for that matter soccer,
was a widely followed sport.

Not until noon did the sky finally clear up a bit,
the hobgoblins crawled back into their holes,
as the radio broadcast the farm report,
the newspaper carried news of war,
of war to come, and yet everything and everyone was fast asleep,
their stomachs filled with lunch,
and the Passerby, too,
took a little nap,
took a little nap,
and this was the dream he had:

He dreamed that he was traveling with his mother, his fifteen-years-deceased
mother, in a little car for the crippled, on a long trip to the other side of "the Curtain."

za ním. Byl před matkou, v jejím klíně, jako by ho právě byla porodila. Ostatně tak spolu jezdili celý život. Přijeli na hranice, celní prohlídka. Vedoucím skupiny celníků byl lékař. Začaly zvláštní ceremonie, při nichž nejprve jeden z členů pohraniční stráže, který držel v ruce jakousi tyčinku, jako by chtěl Kolemjdoucímu vypíchnout oko. Na obranu svého oka udělal Kolemjdoucí rukama rychlý reflexivní pohyb. V téže chvíli se snažil jiný celník strčit Kolemjdoucímu zavařovací teploměr do řitního otvoru. (Měřit teplotu?) Kolemjdoucí udělal rukama stejný pohyb, chránící řitní otvor. Ale už při tomto druhém útoku si začal uvědomovat, že je to všecko jenom jakési strašení, jímž má pohraniční stráž zjistit reakce cestujících. Celník se totiž nijak zvlášť nesnažil. Spokojil se s tím, že se symbolicky dotkl teploměrem řitního otvoru Kolemjdoucího. Přesto měl Kolemjdoucí strach. I tak se lehce mohlo stát nějaké neštěstí. Ten první si například počínal tak neopatrně, že mohl někomu oko skutečně vypíchnout. A také se to jistě už mnohokrát stalo. Ale co záleželo celníkům na nějakém oku? Oko sem, oko tam. Byli to úředníci vykonávající svoji povinnost. Kolemjdoucímu se vynořila nová domněnka, o níž však současně tušil, že je směšně fantastická: Chtějí tak zjišťovat, kdo byl partyzán a kdo ne. Přitom ale nevěděl, které příznaky mluví pro a které proti. Buďto byl partyzán ten, kdo má rychlé reakce: kdo je bystrý, ostražitý. Nebo naopak, příliš úzkostlivé chránící pohyby znamenají bázlivost, labilní nervovou soustavu: Nemohl to být partyzán, partyzán by byl otrlejší. Potom přišla na řadu další procedura. Řekli Kolemjdoucímu a jeho matce, že jim uříznou nohu. Měli na to už připravený přístroj. Zdálo se, že se všecko úplně jasně obrací v žertovnou záležitost. Pokud by byl měl přístroj sloužit k amputaci nohou, byla to směšná hračka: Byl dřevěný a jeho obě „ostří" byla široká skoro půl metru. Horní se mohlo otáčením kliky pohybovat k dolnímu pevnému. Bylo to něco jako ruční lis. Ovšem noha by mohla být rozdrcena. Nesmysl. Lékař a celníci neměli tak krvežíznivé vzezření. Bylo to hra. Kolemjdoucí měl pocit, že už mu někdo o tom vyprávěl: Až tam pojedete, budou vám chtít *jakoby* uříznout nohu. To je jenom legrace. Tento pocit (pocit, že už o tom slyšel) neznamenal, jak si Kolemjdoucí uvědomoval, že mu to někdo vyprávěl skutečně. (Skutečností rozumíme skutečnost jeho snu.) Mohlo to být něco jako „l'illusion du déja vu". Přesně tedy: déja entendu. Totiž: entendu parler. Obrátil se

The Passerby sat in front, driving, his mother behind him. He was in front of his mother, between her legs, as if she were just giving birth to him. As a matter of fact they had driven together that way all their lives. They came to the border, customs inspection. The chief customs inspector was a medical doctor. A series of strange ceremonies ensued, with one of the border patrol agents brandishing a stick, as if he had in mind to poke the Passerby's eye out. In defense of his eye, the Passerby made a quick reflexive gesture with his hands. At the same time another customs inspector tried to poke a jam thermometer into his anal orifice. (To take his temperature?) The Passerby made the same gesture with his hands, protecting his anus. At the second assault, however, he began to realize that the whole thing was some sort of scare tactic meant to establish the travelers' reactions. The customs inspector, you see, didn't really try all that hard, satisfying himself with a token touch of the thermometer to the Passerby's anus. All the same, the Passerby was frightened. There might easily have been an accident. The first agent, for instance, was so careless he might actually have poked somebody's eye out. No doubt it had happened before, and more than once. But what was one eye more or less to the customs inspectors? An eye here, an eye there. They were officials discharging their duties. Albeit he had the feeling it was ridiculously farfetched, a new theory surfaced in the Passerby's mind: The inspectors sought to establish who was a member of the Resistance and who was not. Still, he had no idea which signs meant yes and which meant no. Perhaps the resisters were those who had quick reactions; who were alert, on their guard. Or, on the contrary, perhaps any excessively anxious, defensive movements signified fearfulness, unsteady nerves: Such a person could hardly belong to the Resistance; Resistance fighters were more hardened than that. Next followed another procedure. The officials told the Passerby and his mother that they were going to chop off a leg from each of them. The contraption was right there, ready to go. It was totally obvious that the whole affair was turning into one big practical joke. The contraption that was supposedly meant to amputate their legs was a preposterous toy: It was made of wood, and both of its "cutting edges" were nearly one and a half feet wide. The upper one moved toward the lower one, which was fixed, by turning a crank, a bit like a manual press. It could of course have crushed a leg. But nonsense. Neither the doctor nor the customs inspectors had such a bloodthirsty air about them. It was a game. The Passerby had a feeling that somebody had once told him about it: "When you get there, they pretend that they're going to chop off your leg. It's only a joke." This feeling (the feeling that he had heard about it before) did not mean, the Passerby came to realize, that someone had in reality told him about it. (By "reality" we mean the reality of his dream.) It may have been an illusion of *déjà vu*. Or, to be more precise, *déjà entendu*. That is to say, *entendu parler*. The Passerby turned to his mother and said

k matce a řekl jí francouzsky, aby nerozuměli: Pochopil jsem smysl této zkoušky. Aby nerozuměli? Hloupost. O něco níž přece věděl, že lékař jistě umí francouzsky. Řekl to tedy, aby dal najevo, že není tak hloupý, a potom aby se pochlubil svou franštinou. Ve skutečnosti to bylo z ješitnosti. Uvědomoval si dokonce, že lékař poznal i to. Lékař věděl, že Kolemjdoucí ví, že on (lékař) pochopil pravé motivy jeho výroku. Kolemjdoucí věděl, že lékař ví, že Kolemjdoucí ví, že on (lékař) pochopil pravé motivy jeho výroku. A tak dál až do nekonečna. Do nekonečna v jednom okamžiku. Věděli o sobě všecko, ale nesměli to dát najevo. Podle pravidel jakési hry. Aby mohli žít ve společnosti, aby mohli vykonávat svoje zaměstnání. Lékař zaměstnání vedoucího celní a pasové kontroly a zaměstnání otce rodiny, Kolemjdoucí zaměstnání kolemjdoucího. Aby svět žil, aby lidská společnost mohla existovat. Kolemjdoucího se zmocnil pocit trapnosti. Ještě také z docela jiných důvodů. Napadlo mu totiž, že věta „Pochopil jsem smysl této zkoušky" vypadá jako vytržená z nějaké banální, rádoby mystické katolické literatury. Vzápětí však následoval pocit jisté úlevy. Vzpomněl si, že se spletl a řekl „examen" místo „épreuve". Tím padalo jakékoli podezření z falešného patosu. Pocit blamáže se vynořil hned za pocitem úlevy. Nebo se vynořily všecky tyto pocity současně? Když člověk rozkládá, vypomáhá si různými podvůdky. Například líčí simultánní děje jako následné. Děje! Jako by nešlo o děj jeden, kulovitý a celistvý. Když člověk rozkládá, musí se neustále vracet a opravovat. Neustále musí se všech stran tlačit unikající, nesmírnou odstředivou silou odpuzovaná slova do středu, tj. k tomu, co má být vysloveno. Kuličky mu unikají pod prsty, vrací je znovu, z jiné strany, ale už mu naproti teče do maňásku. Kdo je líný, vzdá se Sisyfovy práce, řekne nějakou duchaplnost o nevýslovnu a že jen hudba může vysloviti vše. Je to pravda stará a dojemná, hodící se do dívčích památníků. Ostatně i slova mají schopnost vytvářet útvary obracející se ke kulovitému chápání. Už moje tetička Maxi (babiččina sestřenice, manželka strýčka Rudiho, který byl c. k. důstojníkem a zemřel ve Štýrském Hradci) říkala, že básni se musí rozumět citem a ne rozumem. Byl jsem rád, protože dál se o tom nemluvilo, a moje nesrozumitelné básně tím byly omluveny. Tetička Maxi hrála hru a umožňovala mi tak pobyt v lidské společnosti. Naproti tomu strýček Rudi, který byl pokrokového smýšlení, říkal, že jednou budou básním rozumět všichni. Také

to her, in French, so the officials would not understand: "I have grasped the meaning of this trial." Not understand? Fiddlesticks. Underneath, the Passerby was well aware that the doctor knew French. The reason he had said it, then, was to make clear that he was no fool, as well as to show off his knowledge of French. In reality it had been out of conceitedness. What's more, he realized that the doctor could see that as well. The doctor knew that the Passerby knew that he (the doctor) had grasped the true motives behind his statement. The Passerby knew that the doctor knew that the Passerby knew that he (the doctor) had grasped the true motives behind his statement. And so on, into infinity. Into infinity in a single instant. They knew everything about one another but weren't allowed to show it. Those were the rules of the game. The rules that made it possible to live in society, to practice their occupations: the doctor, the occupation of chief customs and passport inspector, as well as head of the family; the Passerby, the occupation of passerby. So the world could live, so that human society could exist. The Passerby was overcome with embarrassment. For entirely other reasons as well. For it occurred to him that the sentence "I have grasped the meaning of this trial" sounded as if plucked from some trite, pseudomystic Catholic text. Immediately, however, ensued a feeling of relief, as the Passerby realized he had made a mistake, saying *examen* instead of *épreuve*. This being the case, he could hardly be suspected of false pathos. Directly on the heels of the feeling of relief came the feeling of having lost face. Or did all of these feelings emerge simultaneously? When we analyze, we employ all sorts of little tricks. For instance, we describe simultaneous events as sequential. Events! As if it were not a matter of one single event, globular and whole. When we analyze, we must constantly review and revise. We must from all sides constantly force our escaping words, repelled by immense centrifugal force, back toward the center, i.e., toward that which is to be expressed. As the globules escape our grasp, we send them back again and again, each time from a different side, but meanwhile, across the way, our boat has sprung a leak. The lazy ones renounce this Sisyphean labor, making some witty remark about the ineffable and how music alone is capable of expressing all things. This is an old and heartwarming truism, suitable for the diaries of proper young ladies. For that matter, words too have the capacity to create forms conducive to a globular understanding. For instance my aunt Maxi (cousin of my grandmother and wife of my uncle Rudi, who was an officer in the Austro-Hungarian army and met his death in Graz) used to say that poetry must be understood with the heart and not the head. That made me happy because nothing more was said about it, and my incomprehensible poems were thereby excused. Aunt Maxi was playing a game that made it possible for me to abide in human society. On the other hand, my uncle Rudi, a progressive-thinking man, used to say that there would come a day when everyone would be able to understand poetry. He too

strýček Rudi hrál hru. Neříkám, že vědomky. Někdy mi tetička Maxi citovala Schillera „An die Muse":

Was ich ohne dich wäre, ich weiss es nicht—aber mir grauet,
seh' ich, was ohne dich Hundert' und Tausende sind.

A poklepávala mi významně na rameno, jako že já nejsem bez té múzy. Strýček Rudi si mi stěžoval, že tetička mluví velice často ze sna a říká vždy jednu a tutéž větu: „André Chénier hat dem ewigen Geklapper des Alexandriners ein Ende bereitet". Přitom mívá prý, jak si strýček ve světle stolní lampičky mnohokrát všiml, na tváři blažený úsměv nesmírné úlevy. Poněvadž se tyto noční scény věčně opakovaly, strýček Rudi tomu říkal „das ewige Geklapper des dem ewigen Geklapper des Alexandriners ein Ende bereitenden André Chénier". Tvářil se u toho jako všichni poněkud omezení muži praktického života, hrubě ironizující ušlechtilé zájmy svých daleko jemnějších a o mnoho je převyšujících nepochopených žen.—

Kolemjdoucí se snažil omluvit si v duchu svoji záměnu „examen" a „épreuve" a říkal si: Spletl jsem se. Není divu. Ve spánku! Znamenalo to, že si Kolemjdoucí uvědomuje, že spí? Ne. Znamenalo to, že se mu *zdálo*, že spí. Zdálo se mu (měl sen, byl to obsah jeho snu), že při tom všem, při cestě na hranice Opony, při řízení vozíku pro mrzáky a při celní prohlídce, že při tom všem spí. Byl to v jistém smyslu vnější zásah do obsahu jeho snu, můžeme-li fakt spánku, obestírajícího mozek a celé tělo Kolemjdoucího, považovat za skutečnost vnější a děj jeho snu za skutečnost vnitřní. Vlivem toho, že spal, se mu zdálo, že *spí*, tak jako prý noha vystrčená v zimě v chladném pokoji zpod peřiny může způsobit sen o Severní točně, nebo jako plný močový měchýř vyvolává trapný sen, v němž neustále marně hledáme místo, kde bychom šli na stranu. Situace Kolemjdoucího a jeho matky vypadala chvíli hrozivě, protože lékař se velmi zachmuřil. Kolemjdoucí se rychle snažil smazat trapnost urážky, kterou mu způsobil tím, že podceňoval jeho jazykové znalosti (ačkoliv, jak víme, Kolemjdoucí věděl, že lékař ví, že vlastně nepodceňoval; ale to bylo mimo hru a o tom, co je mimo hru, se nikdy nemluví, všecko se musí odehrát v rovině hry a v této rovině měl lékař právo býti uražen) a začal s lékařem

was playing a game. Perhaps not consciously. Sometimes Aunt Maxi would quote from Schiller's *"An die Muse"*:

> *Was ich ohne dich wäre, ich weiss es nicht—aber mir grauet,*
> *seh' ich, was ohne dich Hundert' und Tausende sind.*

Then she would give me a meaningful pat on the back, to let me know that I was not without a muse. Uncle Rudi would complain that my aunt very often talked in her sleep, and that she always said the very same sentence: *"André Chénier hat dem ewigen Geklapper des Alexandriners ein Ende bereitet."* As she spoke she had on her face, my uncle noticed by the light of the bedside lamp many times, a blissful smile of supreme relief. Seeing as this nighttime scene repeated without end, Uncle Rudi came to refer to it as *"das ewige Geklapper des dem ewigen Geklapper des Alexandriners ein Ende bereitetenden André Chénier."* This he would say wearing the expression of all practical men, being somewhat narrow-minded, when referring in grossly sarcastic tones to the high-minded interests of their far more refined and in many regards superior, yet misunderstood, wives.

The Passerby sought to excuse his confusion between *examen* and *épreuve*, telling himself, "I made a mistake. Hardly surprising. In my sleep!" Did that mean the Passerby was aware that he was asleep? No. It meant that he had *dreamed* he was asleep. He had dreamed (he had a dream, the contents of his dream were) that through it all—the trip to the border of the Curtain, driving the car for the crippled, undergoing the customs inspection—through it all, he had been asleep. It was in a sense an external encroachment on the contents of his dream, provided that we may in fact consider sleep, enveloping the Passerby's brain and entire body, to be the external reality, and the events in his dream to be the internal reality. Owing to the fact that he was sleeping, the Passerby *dreamed* he was asleep, just as a foot sticking out from under a comforter in a cold room in winter may cause one to have a dream about the North Pole, or a full bladder may bring about a distressing dream in which we search in vain for a place to relieve ourselves. For a moment, given the scowl on the doctor's face, the situation for the Passerby and his mother looked grim. Quickly the Passerby sought to erase the embarrassment he felt at having insulted the doctor by underestimating his knowledge of languages (even though, as we know, the Passerby knew that the doctor knew that he had actually done no such thing; this, however, was outside the framework of the game, and what is outside the framework of the game is never spoken of; everything must be played out within the game's framework, and within this framework the doctor had every right to be insulted), launching into a discussion with the doctor on the matter,

mluvit o téže věci docela otevřeně jazykem, jemuž rozuměli oba. Nemohu říci česky, ani nemohu jmenovat nějaký určitý jazyk, protože mluvíme-li s někým ve snu, většinou —nejedná-li se zrovna o nějaké podtržené výroky, nehrají-li slova sama nějakou zvláštní roli, jako tomu bylo v případě oné francouzské věty—zdá se nám pouze smysl našeho rozhovoru, smysl, který by teprve musel být do jazyka přeložen. Dialog ve snu je dialog předjazykový, dialog myšlený, nikoli ve slovech a větách, ale globálně. Proto jistá česká filmová herečka-kolaborantka, která prý se chlubila svému německému manželovi, že se jí už zdají německé sny, a považovala to za doklad toho, jakou dobrou Němkou se stala, bezděky tím právě prozrazovala, že zůstává cizinkou: Sny *německé* (německy mluvené) se jí mohly zdát jenom proto, že si stále uchovávala svoji mateřštinu jako pozadí. Naproti tomu obyčejným příslušníkům toho kterého národa se nezdají sny portugalské, dánské, finské nebo rétorománské, nýbrž prostě *sny*, pokud jazyková stránka sama není na jejich ději nějak zúčastněna. V našem konkrétním případě byl rozhovor, který se Kolemjdoucí honem snažil navázat s lékařem, pokud jde o jazyk, určen ve vědomí spáčově jenom negativně: Na rozdíl od francouzštiny, která ve snu vystupovala jako jazyk cizí, byl to prostě jazyk *necizí*. Kolemjdoucí se utěšoval v duchu: Může si myslet, že jsem zvyklý mluvit s matkou francouzsky. A začal něco, schválně úplně lhostejného, vykládat matce znovu francouzsky, asi tak, jako když někdo pustí ve společnosti hlasitý vítr a pak se rychle snaží vyloudit podobný zvuk podpatkem o linoleum. Linoleum sice vydává podobné zvuky, ale nepáchne. Lékař samozřejmě prohlédl tento manévr. Kolemjdoucí přece věděl, že jej prohlédne. Ale tvrdošíjně se snažil hrát. Napětí trošku povolilo, ale doktor nepřiznal, že se jedná o nějakou „zkoušku". Podle úředních předpisů to patrně žádnému cestujícímu přiznat nesměl. Nebo snad z prestižních důvodů—ale zřejmě už jen formálně—ještě předstíral, že je to všecko vážné. Řekl mírně: Uřízneme vám každému jenom kousek nohy. Jestliže tedy Kolemjdoucí věděl, že se jedná o „zkoušku"—už naprosto bez jakýchkoli pochyb—, nevěděl stále ještě, jak se má chovat, aby se dostal přes hranice. (Smysl „zkoušky" tedy přece jen neznal, chlubil se neprávem.) Buďto neohroženě trvat na tom, že ví, že je to hra, tj. projevit chytrost. Nebo loajálně hrát s sebou i „zkoušku". Byl na strašných rozpacích. Nevěděl, co se od něho očekává. A nejhorší: Při vší té jistotě, že se jedná o zkoušku, měl přece jen strach. Jako když někdo slyší větu: „Buďte rád, že jste nedostal spalničky", a rychle to zaklepává, ačkoli přece není

in a language fully comprehensible to them both. I cannot say it was Czech, nor can I name any other specific language, because when we speak with someone in a dream, for the most part—unless the exchange consists of italicized statements, unless the words themselves play some special role, as in the case of said sentence in French—we dream only the *meaning* of our conversation, which must then still be translated into language. The dialogue of a dream is prelingual; a dialogue thought globally, rather than in words and sentences. This is why a certain Czech film actress and Nazi collaborator, who boasted to her German husband that she had begun to dream in German, believing it to be proof of what a good German she had become, unwittingly revealed in doing so that she remained a foreigner. For she could only have had German dreams (dreams spoken in German) if she were still preserving her mother tongue in the background. By contrast, ordinary members of any given nationality do not have Portuguese, Danish, Finnish, or Rhaeto-Romanic dreams; unless the action of the dream somehow involves language itself, they simply *dream*. In this particular instance, the conversation that the Passerby so hastily sought to strike up with the doctor, insofar as language is concerned, was defined only negatively in the mind of the sleeper: Unlike French, which appeared in the dream as a foreign language, it was simply a *nonforeign* language. The Passerby sought to reassure himself: 'Maybe he thinks I'm accustomed to speaking French with my mother.' And again he began speaking to his mother in French, intentionally saying something completely innocuous, as when someone loudly breaks wind in the middle of a party and then quickly tries to produce a similar sound by rubbing the sole of his shoe against the linoleum floor. Linoleum does of course produce a similar sound; but it doesn't stink. It goes without saying, then, that the doctor saw through this ploy. The Passerby knew very well that he would. In his stubbornness, however, he went on with his act. The tension relaxed somewhat, but the doctor refused to admit it was a "trial" of any sort. Apparently, regulations did not permit him to do so. Or perhaps it was a matter of prestige—even if clearly only pro forma—for the doctor to go on pretending it was all a serious matter. In a gentle tone of voice, he said: "From each of you we shall chop off only a piece of your leg." If the Passerby now knew that it was only a "trial"—at this point, beyond any shadow of a doubt—still he did not know what to do in order to get across the border. (In fact he still didn't understand the point of the "trial," despite his boast to the contrary.) Either he could go on insisting, undaunted, that he knew it was only a game, thereby demonstrating his shrewdness, or he could faithfully continue to play along. The Passerby was at a total loss. He didn't know what was expected of him. And worst of all, despite his certainty it was a trial, he was still afraid. As when somebody hears the sentence "Just be glad you've never had the measles," and quickly knocks on wood, even if he is not nearly so foolish as to believe that he can ward off

tak hloupý, aby si myslel, že zaklepání může zažehnat spalničky. A přece jenom má strach nezaklepat. Unberufen toi, toi, toi. Il faut toucher le bois. Kolemjdoucí zasunoval nohu pomalu a bázlivě do aparátu, šikmo, takže trošku ucítil jednu hranu dolního špalku, na niž se jeho lýtko lehce přitisklo. Věděl docela určitě, že se nemůže pořezat, a přece měl pocit, jako by strkal nohu mezi samé žiletky. Konečně zaťal zuby a položil ji prudce na dolní špalek.

Rozhodl se hrát až do konce.

Potom večer,
když Kolemjdoucí seděl u stolu
a slyšel
bzučet přes celé nebe až do parků
několik Mléčných drah
blanokřídlého hmyzu,
jeho bytná vešla do pokoje,
nesla mu ukázat
zelenou vážku, jejíž jméno nezná,
kdopak se může vyznat v blanokřídlých,
kdopak zná všechen blanokřídlý hmyz!

A také já jsem tam seděl,
ve čtvrtém poschodí,
o třicet schodů výš, pode mnou Kolemjdoucí,
a kdybych vyšel z vrat,
ulice, domy, chodci,
kdopak zná všechen blanokřídlý hmyz,
ten bzukot ale znám, a úplný,
veliký, kulovitý…
Vtom jeden z přátel na mne zapískal,
průvodčí zvoní, jedou funebráci,
ulice, domy, chodci a tak dál.

Nic víc než nosit svět
jak bludný balvan v hlavě
jsem tady neuměl a to je asi málo,
tak jako v čínských básních

the measles by knocking on wood. And yet, he is afraid not to. *Unberufen toi, toi, toi. Il faut toucher du bois.* Slowly, gingerly, the Passerby inserted his leg into the contraption; sideways, so that he felt one edge of the lower block pressing lightly against his calf. He was quite sure he would not be cut, and yet he had the feeling he was sticking his leg in between a pair of razor blades. Finally he gritted his teeth and brought his leg down sharply on the lower block.

He had made up his mind to play it out to the end.

Then in the evening,
as the Passerby sat down at the table
and heard
the buzzing of several milky ways
of hymenopterans,
all across the sky and down into the parks,
his landlady entered the room,
coming to show him
a green dragonfly whose name she did not know,
who can tell all of those insects apart, anyway,
who knows the names of all of those bees and wasps and ants?!

And I too was sitting there,
there on the fourth floor,
thirty steps higher, with the Passerby beneath me,
and if I had walked out the door,
the streets, the buildings, the people out walking,
who knows the names of all of those bees and wasps and ants,
the buzzing, though, I know; whole,
enormous, globular…
Just then, one of my friends whistled to me,
the conductor is ringing, the pallbearers are on the way,
the streets, the buildings, the people out walking, and so on.

To carry the world around,
like the stone of Sisyphus, in my head
this was all I knew how to do and that is very little,
just as in Chinese poetry

je toho někdy málo,
nic víc než obloha, po které letí pták,
po které letí pták, ale ten opravdový,
co přestal hrát už hru, co už si nehraje,
a za to málo, za to strašně málo
dám nohu na špalek,
tak jako Kolemjdoucí,
tak jako Kolemjdoucí,
jenomže naopak.

there is sometimes very little,
nothing more than the sky and a bird flying across it,
a bird flying across it; a bird, but a real one,
one that has ceased to play the game, one that will play no more,
and for that little thing, a thing next to nothing
I would put my leg on the block,
just like the Passerby,
just like the Passerby,
only the other way round.

from

OLD ADDRESSES (1979)

TRANSLATED BY JUSTIN QUINN & MATTHEW SWENEY

STARÁ BYDLIŠTĚ

6, Brunswick Gardens, Kensington

Maqui, můj kocourku, co děláš, ještě žiješ?
Musíš být velmi stár a znaven, jak je ti?
Je ještě v knihovně ta krásná poezie,
jsou ještě v knihovně Štolbovy paměti?

Brunšvické zahrady. Princ Albert ještě žije,
v Hyde Parku, v Kensingtnu, zde v těchto zahradách.
A žije starý dvůr, a žije Viktorie,
umíme setřít prach, umíme setřít prach.

Žije jak Chittussi, jak Štolba na jevišti,
žije jak minulé, žije jak všichni příští,
žije, jak v Anglii ožívá národ náš.

Pouť budoucí je tvá, zbavena zemské tíhy,
pouť budoucí je tvá, obrazy, básně, knihy,
pouť budoucí je tvá, a ty ji uhlídáš.

OLD ADDRESSES

6, Brunswick Gardens, Kensington

Maqui, my tomcat! Still at your old ways?
You must be awfully tired by now. What's up?
Are all those lovely poems still in the case?
Are Štolba's memoirs still there on the top?

Brunswick Gardens. Prince Albert's still alive.
In Hyde Park, Kensington, the old court must
still be alive, of course and Albert's wife.
Oh we can clean the dust, oh clean the dust.

Like Chittussi lives and Štolba's on the stage
just like before, just like a future age.
He lives. In England, our land lives again.

And you will wander, with no earthly weight.
And you will wander, poems & books for freight.
And you will wander, guarding what remains.

[JQ]

PODZIM

Shrabovat listí v parcích, jaká klidná práce.
Přecházet sem a tam a pomalu se vracet,
jako se vrací čas, jako se vrací dálka,
nostalgická jak známky na obálkách.

Našel jsem dopis, jenom tužkou psaný,
smazaný deštěm, zpola roztrhaný.

Ó dobo dopisů, kde jsi, kde jsi?
Jak Rilke psal jsem dlouhé dopisy;
teď mlčím, sbohem, přišel listopad.
Ryšaví koně vyjíždějí z vrat.

AUTUMN

Raking leaves in the park, what could be better.
To go here and there, slow to return,
as time returns, as distance returns too,
nostalgic like stamps on a letter.

I found a letter, written only in lead,
rain worn, half torn.

O epistolary era, where have you fled?
I have written long letters as Rilke used to;
no more, farewell, it's November, late.
The red horses are out of the gate.

[MS]

NEDĚLE

Je neděle Mám volno
pacienti očekávají své návštěvníky
chodím mezi budovou nemocnice a farmou
snad budu mít také nějakou návštěvu
snad mě najdou
snad se na cestě objeví Brušák
anebo Listopad
anebo Dresler
jsou tady v cizině léta a ještě jsem je neviděl
mám připraveny básně
budeme mluvit o literatuře
svět bude zase plný života.

SUNDAY

It's Sunday I have the day free
the patients await their visitors
I go back and forth between the hospital building and the farm
maybe I'll have a visitor too
maybe they'll find me
maybe Brušák will show up on the road
or Listopad
or Dresler
they've been abroad here for years and I still haven't seen them
I have poems ready
we'll talk about literature
the world will be full of life again.

[MS]

HODINY VODNÉ

Ladný řetěz golfových klubů se vine zahradami
Vše je zaskleno

Zdá se že tento skleník je Anglie
Neustále je vidět kolik je ve vzduchu vody
Paměť ryb je nikdy neopustila

Kde bychom mohli bydlet v Československu?
Snad ve Vrchlabí
přímo u řeky.

WATER CLOCK

An elegant chain of country clubs meanders through the gardens
Everything is glassed in

It seems as though this greenhouse is England
You can always see how much water is in the air
The memory of fish never left them

Where could we live in Czechoslovakia?
Perhaps in Vrchlabí
right on the river.

[MS]

NOC

Posádka spí
Osvobození zajatci mají manévry

Když vyspravili roury u kamen v bombami poškozených domech
nasadili si cylindry
Mrtví obyvatelé se usmáli
Mrtví obyvatelé měli krásný sen.

NIGHT

The garrison sleeps
The freed prisoners of war are out on maneuvers

When they fixed the stovepipes in the bomb-blasted houses
they put their stovepipe hats on
The dead inhabitants smiled
The dead inhabitants had pleasant dreams.

[MS]

NOKTURNO

V noci, když se rozsvěcuje obilí
v sýpkách měsíčního světla,
každé zrnko ovsa svítí zvlášť.
Čarodějnice usedají na pometla.

Onen podivín z vesnice, který si myslí, že nikdy nezemře,
vstává a odchází směrem k Morton-Morell.
Jdu kousek s ním, doprovázím ho.
Potkáváme dva letní hosty.

NOCTURNE

At night, when wheat glows
in granaries lit by the moon,
each grain of oat shines brightly.
Witches stride their brooms.

One loony from the village, who thinks he'll never die,
gets up and heads for Morton-Morell.
I go a ways with him, keep him company.
We meet two summer guests.

[MS]

CIGARETA

Klementu Bochořákovi

Když člověk zapálí po práci cigaretu,
úlevný lehký smích se vkrádá do údů.
Úlevný lehký smích, a kuřák dává světu
přiznání dobrých chvil, dobrého osudu.

Bzukote nádraží a telegrafních drátů,
pošli mi ještě tam, kde Halas kouříval,
pošli mi pozdravy k Březinům do Kunštátu,
na nízký Anaberk, jen o kousíček dál.

Vydech jsem modrý kouř a modrý kouř se nese
do vašich Pisárek. Myslím si, že jsem v lese,
vracím se zpátky zas brněnskou tramvají.

Jedeme do remíz a kolem výstaviště,
kde vzadu za věží je fotbalové hříště,
jedeme na hřbitov a dívky mávají.

CIGARETTE

for Klement Bochořák

When a man lights up after his work is done,
a grinning lightness steals through every limb.
A grinning lightness, and all his burdens gone—
he grants that life is sometimes good to him.

O trains and telegraph lines all abuzz,
send me back there where Halas smoking stood.
Send my best to Kunštát and the Březinas,
and Anaberk a small bit down the road.

Blue smoke I blew out and blue smoke now floats
to your Pisárky. I think I'm in the woods.
Once more, a Brno tramcar takes me there.

We're going through the trees. We're swinging round
the Expo and beyond the football ground
to the cemetery, and girls wave in the air.

[JQ]

PODZIM III

Ach, kam se poděla všecka má krásná léta,
mé krásné předsíně před byty sladkých žen,
šelesty, chodidla a okouzlení světa,
ó proč jsem zůstal sám, sám, sám a samoten.

Jak mrtvá bohyně sad zachvěl se a pad',
pohřební zaměstnanci vynášejí máry,
hrad zůstal stát, hrad zůstal stát
a kolem letí cáry.

Města a vesničky v podzimním tichu spící,
když herci vybalí své šminky na stanici,
zvedne se opona, orchestr začne hrát.

Ředitel Nádhera přechází v zákulisí,
ředitel Červíček zas zpívá jako kdysi
a hvězda odchází, zas jako tolikrát.

AUTUMN III

All my lovely years, where have they whirled,
those lovely hallways that led to sweet women,
the murmurs, ankles, the magic of the world?
Oh why did I stay alone, alone, alone?

The orchard shook and fell like a dead goddess.
The undertakers usher out the bier.
The castle stands, oh nonetheless,
and shreds fly far and near.

The villages drowse in the autumn plains
while actors take their greasepaint off the train
The curtain rises. The band begins to play.

Nádhera the director paces backstage,
Červíček sings as in a bygone age,
and stars depart again, the same old way.

[JQ]

FOTBAL

Vladimíru Bařinovi

V malebném zákoutí u malé řeky Svratky,
Meteor VIII tady kdysi hrál.
Byla to remíza. Ó vraťte se mi zpátky,
Řitičko, Vršecký, Paráčku a tak dál.

Chci delší zápasy, zápas je příliš krátký.
Osudná píšťalka a ty bys ještě stál
u brány fotbalu, fotbalu, naší matky,
a zatím zkoušíš už kolotoč opodál…

Déšť stírá labutě na mokrém kolotoči,
déšť stírá myslivce a panny krásných očí,
střelnice umlkly, houpačky musí stát.

Moravská Slavie je kdesi v třetí třídě;
a v tomto úkrytu jsem ji už neuviděl,
slyšel jsem jenom vlak u Heršpic zapískat.

Na hřišti pod lesem bude s ní jistě hrát
A. F. C. Marathon, schoulený u Rosničky.
Také tak hluboko, hluboko kdysi spaď,
a teď tam pobíhá s roztrhanými tričky.

Budeme celý zápas sledovat
z daleké Anglie za zavřenými víčky.
Na této televizi uvidíme snad
penalty, ofsajdy a nemotorné kličky.

Tam vidět fanoušky a jejich pěstní hádky,
tam zůstat, zůstat tam – zápas je příliš krátký –
pod celou kupou klubů vyšších tříd.

Tam zůstat, zůstat tam, poblíže řeky Svratky,
poblíže fotbalu, fotbalu, naší matky,
a nemuset se narodit.

FOOTBALL

for Vladimír Bařina

In a pleasant dell along the River Svratka,
Meteor VIII once played. The contest
was a draw. O take me back, Řitička,
Vršecký, Paráček, and the rest.

If only games were longer! What do you do as
the whistle blows and you're left standing there
on the grounds? Football, like a mother to us.
You wander off and try rides at the fair.

Rain sweeps across the swan on the carousel.
Rain sweeps across the huntsman and the damsel.
The swings and shies went still some time ago.

Our Slavia is in the third division.
They never played here on a single occasion
I only heard a train's far whistle blow.

On the pitch beneath the woods, they'll surely play
AFC Marathon, Rosnička's own.
They fell so far, so far, that now today
they run around in gear that's ripped and worn.

We'll watch the match in its entirety
from far-off England, from behind closed eyes.
On this TV, with any luck we'll see
the offsides and the fouls, the angry cries.

To see the fans fling all kinds of abuse,
to stay for ever longer games, refuse
to climb league-tables, leave the jerseys torn,

to stay, to stay there near the Svratka's sluice,
near football, football, like a mother to us,
and never have been born.

[JQ]

RÝN

Dnes před patnácti léty jsme přejeli Rýn
Apollinaire
Oh saisons oh châteaux
zanechávajíce za sebou zlatým lišejníkem obrostlé rýnské hrady
kde zámecké paní krmí holuby.

THE RHINE

Fifteen years ago today we crossed the Rhine
Apollinaire
Oh saisons oh châteaux
leaving behind us the gold lichen overgrown Rhine castles
where the chateau ladies feed the pigeons.

[MS]

LOUISE

Nákladní auto odjíždí k Montrouge
Proč jsme nebydleli v tomto francouzském městě
pustém jak jatky skoro neobydleném

Mohli jsme myslet že život je smrt
na dalekém předměstí Paříže
na dalekém nepochopitelném předměstí Paříže.

LOUISE

The delivery van departs for Montrouge
Why didn't we live in that French town
deserted like a slaughterhouse almost uninhabited

We could have thought that life is death
in a remote suburb of Paris
in a remote inconceivable suburb of Paris.

[MS]

FROM A TERRACE IN PRAGUE

Můj dědeček byl optik
Kdykoli jsem šel v Československu v nějakém jiném městě kolem optického obchodu
myslel jsem na rodinu jeho majitele

Za Karlovým mostem za Mosteckou věží na Malé Straně
je také optický krám
Snad se jeho majitel vracíval domů přes Kampu
po Mostě legií kolem Národního divadla
snad měl byt v Novodvorské ulici pod Petřínem

Dnes kdy píši tuto báseň Seminářská zahrada kvete a to co Součková vídávala z terasy
se vlní kolébá zní drobnými zvuky od Starých zámeckých schodů k Malé Straně.

FROM A TERRACE IN PRAGUE

My grandfather was an optician
Whenever I went to some other town in Czechoslovakia round the optician's
I thought of the family of its owner

Behind Charles Bridge behind Mostecká Tower in the Lesser Quarter
there is also an optician's
Perhaps the owner used to go home across Kampa Island
over Legionnaires' Bridge around the National Theatre
perhaps he had a flat on Novodvorská Street below Petřín Hill

Today as I write this poem the Seminářská Garden is in bloom, and what Součková used to see
        from the terrace
meanders rocks resounds with tiny sounds from the Old Castle Stairs to the Lesser Quarter.

[MS]

STIMMUNG

Karfiolové skříně budovy
stojí nepohnuty v polích

Pole se táhnou
od stadionu k šekovému úřadu
od šekového úřadu k vojenskému velitelství
od vojenského velitelství k právnické fakultě
od právnické fakulty k hřišti S. K. Žabovřesky.

STIMMUNG

Cauliflower cabinet buildings
stand still in the fields

The fields stretch out
from the stadium to the office of the Treasury
from the Treasury to the military headquarters
from the military headquarters to the law faculty
from the law faculty to the Žabovřesky team's playing field.

[MS]

ZA VIADUKTEM

Nosila podivné předměty z dveří do dveří
neznal jsem ji

Zedníci zpívali přicházelo jaro

Obyvatelé ulice U synagogy hodní románu
vystrkují hlavy z plesnivých oken.

BEHIND THE VIADUCT

She carried strange items from door to door
I did not know her

Bricklayers sang Spring has come

The inhabitants of Synagogue Street, worthy of a novel
stick their heads out of moldy windows.

[MS]

from

BIXLEY REMEDIAL SCHOOL (1979, 1982)

TRANSLATED BY VERONIKA TUCKEROVÁ
AND ANNA MOSCHOVAKIS

LÉON-PAUL FARGUE: DROGA

Nemohu zapomenout na pocit jednoho rána v Alexandra Park
kdy jsem byl úplně spojen s bílými holuby
byli bílí jak sníh

On pán všeho tvorstva stvořil drogu zvanou artein
the drug of art
of modest small old surrealistic art.

LÉON-PAUL FARGUE: A DRUG

I cannot forget the feeling one morning in Alexandra Park
I was completely connected with white pigeons
they were white as snow

He the Lord of all creatures created the drug called artaine
the drug of art
of modest small old surrealistic art.

JANUA SAPIENTIAE

The Monx speak Monx
I speak czech and english
I have an instrument for getting traffic-wordens out of the drain-pipes
and changing them into an apple-rose

It all happens in time-space
when the traffic warden is already out
we can hear the noise.

POHŘEBNÍ HUDBA

Vykřičené domy se hemží zákazníky
pastucha který navštívil město je hledá
ptá se mě na cestu jako v Jiráskově Lucerně
právo světlonoše

You must scrub the floor of the lavatory all naked
on your hands and knees
even melody.

FUNERAL MUSIC

Houses of ill repute swarm with clients
a new shepherd in town is looking for them
he asks me for directions, like in Jirásek's The Lantern
the right of the torchbearer

You must scrub the floor of the lavatory all naked
on your hands and knees
even melody.

SLAVNOST

Poetry is a panacea for all illnesses
bratři Marxové vylupují žloutek

Der Dichter spricht in verschiedenen Sprachen
na dně jezera kde vodníci nocují

Volná cesta byla zatarasena
quite blocked by gaiety girls.

FESTIVITY

Poetry is a panacea for all illnesses
the Marx Brothers pluck the egg yolk out

Der Dichter spricht in verschiedenen Sprachen
on the bottom of the lake where mermen spend the night

The open road was blocked
quite blocked by gaiety girls.

TULÁK SPÍ NA LOUCE

Budižkničemu se toulá po ulicích města
always under pressure of the moral institutes

But he won't go to a borstal
louky die Wiesen na něj čekají za městem

Wie sen jak sen how a dream
zbytečná otázka
stejně si nemohu nic pamatovat.

THE DRIFTER SLEEPS IN THE MEADOW

The good for nothing wanders the city streets
always under pressure of the moral institutes

But he won't go to a borstal
meadows die Wiesen await him outside of the city

Wie dream as dream how a dream
a useless question
no matter I can't remember a thing.

MENUE

Kdyby mě nějaká žena pozvala do „pokoje"
měl bych potom úplně šťastný den
také nemám tolik cigaret jako včera
také nemám tolik cigaret jako včela

Perhaps it is macaroni cheese
I'll go for dinner
there is perhaps the drug called happinesse.

MENUE

If a woman invited me into the "room"
I would have a totally happy day
I also don't have as many cigarettes as yesterday
I also don't have as many cigarettes as a bee

Perhaps it is macaroni cheese
I'll go for dinner
there is perhaps the drug called happinesse.

MODLITBIČKA

Vaječnou omeletu s posekanou šunkou bych snědl
Frede přijď
kolik hodin nám zbývá do noci
také plesnivý Camembert i s kůrkou

Proč se Oslo už nejmenuje Kristiania
toužím po náboženství.

A LITTLE PRAYER

An egg omelette with chopped ham I would eat
come, Fred
how many hours are left till night
and moldy Camembert, with a crust

Why isn't Oslo still called Kristiania?
I crave religion.

DRINK

Nepřijal bych návštěvu do Československa
nesouhlasím s okupací Rudé armády

Ale v Rudé armádě jsou ženy
nothing at all

Dissipate the fears of venereal diseases
with a goblet of rum.

DRINK

I would not accept a visit to Czechoslovakia
I do not agree with the Red Army's occupation

But there are women in the Red Army
nothing at all

Dissipate the fears of venereal diseases
with a goblet of rum.

THIRST

No mice no flies no goblins
perfect life

It may be already quarter to two
David Westbrook appeared

Friends and muchachas
take me to a distant tanking station.

SYSTOLY SE NAPÍNAJÍ A POVOLUJÍ

Nejrůznější systémy organické hmoty chodí oklikami
nechtějí dovnitř a zpět

Vstávejte sladce
mé komplikace

Stačí vám někdy láska pomněnky
k níž se sklání mladý Metuzalém.

THE ARTERIES STRETCH AND RELAX

Organic systems take the long way round
they don't want inside and back

Get up sweetly
my complications

Sometimes the love of a forget-me-not is enough for you
the young Methuselah stoops down to it.

ŠKOLA

Fred has arrived
the evening is ending happily
I got a new pen from the stores
a new old pen
it started to write in the twenties
some of the people of the first manifestoes still live.

SCHOOL

Fred has arrived
the evening is ending happily
I got a new pen from the stores
a new old pen
it started to write in the twenties
some of the people of the first manifestoes still live.

POSLEDNÍ BÁSEŇ 18. ŘÍJNA

I have now two pens and plenty of papers
na inkoust mlsné sny se staví do fronty před jídelnou lásky
dark green ivy is overgrowing the vicarage
všecky jazyky jsou mlsné
na rohu čeká mls
vesele do nového století.

THE LAST POEM OCTOBER 18TH

I have now two pens and plenty of papers
for ink sweet-toothed dreams line up at the dining hall of love
dark green ivy is overgrowing the vicarage
all tongues are sweet-toothed
in the corner the sweet waits
happily into the new century.

FATE

The will to life is remorselessly exploding all eternity
there is no death
we must acquiesce
there is now and then the yes
yes we want it so
we can't choose the absolute nothing.

OUTSIDE AND IN

A group of factory buildings may be called a plant
God the linguist teaches us to breathe

In a hollow of a tree
there is a cart
there lives the wood-cock
there is the crown
there is the flamboyant madame Lupescu.

ANARCHY

There is a village without a bell
there is the world without leadership

Choc-ice is in czech called Eskymo
I used to have three on a bench at Felixtow Road
every Saturday and Sunday

Vážím se jen netto.

ANARCHY

There is a village without a bell
there is the world without leadership

Choc-ice is in czech called Eskymo
I used to have three on a bench at Felixtow Road
every Saturday and Sunday

I weigh myself, but net.

PERHAPS WE CAN pebble at the other side
u živého plotu kde Madame de Chevreuse okusuje listí
come on hirdie
kozy nežijí nikdy v stádech
jedna dvě kozy na celém statku

Potrat žil deset minut
pak matka užívala eumenol
pak matka užívala agomensin
pak matka užívala apuiol

I use salt-peter after shaving
chilský ledek z jižní Ameriky
póry jsou staženy.

PERHAPS WE CAN pebble at the other side
at the hedge where Madame de Chevreuse munches the leaves
come on hirdie
goats never live in herds
one or two goats for the entire farm

The abortion lived for ten minutes
then the mother used eumenol
then the mother used agomensin
then the mother used apuiol

I use salt-peter after shaving
Chilean saltpeter from South America
the pores have tightened up.

SMUTEK

Nebýti těchto pěti stěn,
I'd feel like Role Celestien,

but he didn't take me out,
poor old Solley.

Einsames Bett, traurige Morgenstunden,
die schöne Hochzeit ist verschwunden.

SADNESS

If it weren't for these five walls,
I'd feel like Role Celestien,

but he didn't take me out,
poor old Solley.

Einsames Bett, traurige Morgenstunden,
die schöne Hochzeit ist verschwunden.

NEVER LIGHT THE job
Nottingham is in the North of England
potato blight killed there all the bulbs

Nemám žádná pravidla
o všem zůstávám nerozhodnutý
zůstanu v

There is a church in America
and when you get married
the priest gets more voices
to get to bed in the evening
it is not my birth-day
to expect the triumph of God in the morning

NEVER LIGHT THE job
Nottingham is in the North of England
potato blight killed there all the bulbs

I have no rules
I'm still undecided about everything
I'm still in

There is a church in America
and when you get married
the priest gets more voices
to get to bed in the evening
it is not my birth-day
to expect the triumph of God in the morning

HAPPINESSE

Pursuit of happiness
that's one of the rights of american citizens
granted by the constitution of 1832

What does it mean
it means to marry and have children
or not to have children and have the woman
the woman only

If you haven't got a woman have a dog.

MISSPELLED

So restoration is not spelled *au*
I spelled it so thinking of the czech word restaurace
to restore
and go with a lady to the Room
like a unicorn in the mirror
all naked in the mirrors
so that I could see the blood trickling.

INVALID

Už zase se těším jenom na spánek
oddechl jsem si

V Trapezuntu v Byzancii byl slavný klášter
Říše východořímská
Byzantium je jenom hlavní město
neumím podržet v hlavě celou mapu.

INVALID

Once again, only sleep to look forward to
I had relaxed

In Trapezunt, in Byzantium, there was a famous monastery
The Byzantine Empire
Byzantium is just the capital
I can't hold the whole map in my head.

CESTA JE POSETA HVĚZDAMI

La route est semée d'étoiles
a člověk symbolů jde zšeřelými háji

Nikdy jsem si nemyslel že čmelák může bodnout
malá plstnatá kulička

Je symbolem svatby pro Báseň v cizím bytě
nad městem bzučí letadlo jak čmelák

The guest star is Bing Crosby
the guest star is Bob Hope

The bumble-bee may be also called humble-bee
they humbly suck the nectar
without being able to build a hive.

THE ROAD IS SOWED WITH STARS

La route est semée d'étoiles
and the man of symbols walks through twilit woods

I never thought a bumble bee could sting
a small felt ball

It's the symbol of weddings in the Poem in a Strange Flat
above the city an airplane hums like a bumble-bee

The guest star is Bing Crosby
the guest star is Bob Hope

The bumble-bee may be also called humble-bee
they humbly suck the nectar
without being able to build a hive.

LÁSKA

Python má až tři jazyky v ústech
nejraději mám dva

Včela navštíví pět set květů
než naplní svůj žaludek zvíci špendlíkové hlavičky

Tráví jako Rilke
probably moss which the bumble-bee can't reach

But the wood butterfly's caterpillar does
v zakletém lese plném motýlů

One of them is Rosie
she has a big roman nose.

LOVE

The python has up to three tongues in his mouth
I prefer two

A bee visits five hundred flowers
until she fills her wee stomach

She digests like Rilke
probably moss which the bumble-bee can't reach

But the wood butterfly's caterpillar does
in an enchanted butterfly forest

One of them is Rosie
she has a big roman nose.

ANOTHER POETICAL LESSON

UNCOLLECTED POEMS

Roman Catholic

To pope John Paul the Second

Why shouldn't the a Roman Catholic?
It is so nice to believe in angels
it is so nice to have a pope above
pontifex maximus
Salvator Dali had an audience with
                                            him.

Least said, soon mended.

ROMAN CATHOLIC

To pope John Paul the Second

Why shouldn't I be a Roman Catholic?
It is so nice to believe in angels
it is so nice to have a pope above
pontifex maximus
Salvator Dali had an audience with him.

Least said, soon mended.

Another honor for my saint

Francis of Assisy ~~is~~ has been declared the patron

saint of earth oekology

the cage without frontiers

the sweet community of plants animals and

~~men~~ people

Yes, he was preaching to birds

What about rivers? They are living men

old father Thames is rolling along.

ANOTHER HONOR FOR MY SAINT

Francis of Assisy has been declared the patron saint of earth oekology
the cage without frontiers
the sweet community of plants, animals and people
yes, he was preaching to birds

What about rivers? They are living men
old father Thames is rolling along.

La verre

The pink cover-spring of my first book Daní
wasn't what I expected   jitienka

I wanted to be published exactly like
                                    Baudelaire
like Svata Kadlec Baudelaire

Jeiner be Svata Kadlec,
the lunatic

Translate me into english
I want to be read by Valentine Penrose

In the book it is Penrose and spoils
                              the rhythm

Bronsky budte prstě onahnejší.
                    *

LA VERRE

The pink cover-spring of my first book Paní jitřenka
wasn't what I expected

I wanted to be published exactly like Baudelaire
like Svata Kadlec Baudelaire

Teiner be Svata Kadlec,
the lunatic

Translate me into english
I want to be read by Valentine Penrose

In the book it is Petorose and spoils the rhythm
Brousku, buďte příště opatrnější.

La Verre: "The Glass" (French)
Brousku, buďte příště opatrnější : "Brousek, next time be more careful."

*

Both

If it were morning in the Pines I would take
                                    gun-powder
it's afternoon on Bixley
or at Bixley
the praepositions in english are a trouble

You never made a serious error or blunder
"on" or "at" I think that both are right.

*

BOTH

If it were morning in the Pines I could take gun-powder
it is afternoon on Bixley
or *at* Bixley
the praepositions in english are a trouble

God never made a serious error or blunder
"on" or "at" I think that both are right.

Mizina

The mountains are questioned by the moun-
                        tain-climbers

but there is no answer
there are no disciples
but St. Bernard's dogs will reach you
and tell you at once to return to the
                                        valley
    and never more to climb.

                    *

NÍŽINA

The mountains are questioned by the mountain-climbers
but there is no answer
there are no disciples
but St. Bernard's dogs will reach you
and tell you at once to return to the valley
and never more to climb.

Nížina: "lowland"

High Class

Prince Philip is a great gastronomer
he instructs a brigade of cooks

The archipelago of Palau has the richest
                marine life in all the Pacific
I remember only moluses feeding on algae
uzpominam si jenom na mlže
maji' filtr

Prince Philip wouldn't like to live in
                underseas chambers
he prefers Buckingham Palace and
                the Queen.

She has got one.

                ✳

HIGH CLASS

Prince Philip is a great gastronome
he instructs a brigade of cooks

The archipelago of Palau has the richest marine life in all the Pacific
I remember only molluscs feeding on algae
vzpomínám si jenom na mlže
mají filtr

Prince Philip wouldn't like to live in underseas chambers
he prefers Buckingham Palace and the Queen.
She has got one.

---

vzpomínám si jenom na mlže/mají filtr: "I remember only the molluscs/they have a filter"

*

Ba, Ba, Black Sheep

The mountain black sheep descended
    to the valley but Rosa Bonheur
    can't paint them black is ~~a~~
    the colour of death and there is
    no death in the universe

luckily enough, because I enjoy life
pendling between the table and the te-
        levision

Be quiet sister
a monad can die
I'll stay
a bit selfishly
thinking only of the coloured cover
    of my book on the table in my
        workshop.

BA, BA, BLACK SHEEP

The mountain black sheep descended to the valley but Rosa Bonheur can't paint
        them black is the colour of death and there is no death in the universe
luckily enough, because I enjoy life
pendling between the table and the television

Be quiet sister
a monad can die
I'll stay
a bit selfishly
thinking only of the coloured cover of my book on the table in my workshop.

Příroda

The number of ringlets on the wasp
                    means the number of its
                              marriages
they don't have a queen they mate
                              freely

Eckelhaft sagte die Arbeiterin Biene
and threw out the drone

But he, finding his greatest pleasure in
                              dying
said thank you darling it was
                              worth it.

*

PŘÍRODA

The number of ringlets on the wasp means the number of its marriages
they don't have a queen they mate freely

Eckelhaft sagte die Arbeiterin Biene
and threw out the drone

But he, finding his greatest pleasure in dying
said thank you darling it was worth it.

Příroda: "nature"
Eckelhaft sagte die Arbeiterin Biene: "disgusting, said the worker bee" (German)

*

Come on you lazy censors
confiscate my poem
put a dark oblog in its place
I wanted to say black
black jako na umrtním *vznámení*

COME ON YOU lazy censors
confiscate my poem
put a dark oblong in its place
I wanted to say black
black jako na úmrtním oznámení

---

jako na úmrtním oznámení: "like in the death notice"

*

The end of Eternity

At once I got up
Mr. Rehem was standing by
and sid
that's all right Ivan
ideal morning
a bit of embarrassement before the early tea in the dark
and then a straight road to heaven.

THE END OF ETERNITY

At once I got up
Mr. Rehem was standing by
and said
that's all right Ivan
ideal morning
a bit of embarrassment before the early tea in the dark
and then a straight road to heaven.

Another Poetical Lesson

There are eight kinds of swans in the
                                    world
I know only three

Quite white ones with a black spot round
                                    the beak
quite white ones with a yellow and black
                            spot round the beak
and black and white ones like the famous
                                    whisky
To drink them all and end up down the
                                    Styx.

*

ANOTHER POETICAL LESSON

There are eight kinds of swans in the world
I know only three

Quite white ones with a black spot round the beak
quite white ones with a yellow and black spot round the beak
and black and white ones like the famous whisky

To drink them all and end up down the Styx.

                              *
                        Bad Memory

Drydens Annus Mirabilis was about 1666
the year of the Great London Fire
what shall I say about 1979

The spring was beautiful

Sandy remained in the wheel-chair all year
and Germany has had new Junkers.

BAD MEMORY

Dryden's Annus Mirabilis was about 1666
the year of the Great London Fire
what shall I say about 1979

The spring was beautiful

Sandy remained in the wheel-chair all year
and Germany has had new Junkers.

Walter de la Mare

Das Glocke
dismantled body-leg
ve volných ulicích naproti průcho-
dům

✝

He wasn't lazy, look
he wrote a big fat book

How many poems there are
by Walter de la Mare.

✳

WALTER DE LA MARE

Das Glocke
dismanteled body-leg
ve volných ulicích naproti průchodům

He wasn't lazy, look
he wrote a big fat book

How many poems there are
by Walter de la Mare.

---

die Glocke: "bell" (German). Blatný's use of the definite article *das* is incorrect.
ve volných ulicích naproti průchodům: "in the empty streets opposite the passageways"

In Memoriam

Walter de la Mare died 1956
the year of the hungarian uprising
so he won't read my old-fashioned
                                    poems

Was he a Londoner?
Did he live in the country?
Why had we to lose him in the
                                    maze.

                    *

IN MEMORIAM

Walter de la Mare died 1956
the year of the hungarian uprising
so he won't read my old-fashioned poems

Was he a Londoner?
Did he live in the country?
Why had we to lose him in the maze.

Queen, drones, bee-workers, zivot vcel
thatis the beehives personelle

Now I must whisper in low tone
Iwas today a dying drone

But Ia m fresh and Glück—alive
back in the vil, back in the hive.

*

QUEEN, DRONES, BEE-WORKERS, život včel
that is the bee hive's personnel

Now I must whisper in low tone
I was today a dying drone

But I am fresh and Glück-alive
back in the úl, back in the hive.

život včel: "the life of bees" / *Glück:* "happy" (German) / *úl:* "hive"

Afterword

In the beginning of the 1970s, the concerts of Vlasta Třešňák, Jaroslav Hutka and Vladimír Merta were some of the last remnants of publicly accesible uncensored Czech culture. During these concerts, Miroslav Kovařík would recite the poems of important Czech and foreign authors. Among his top performances were those of the texts of the American beatniks (Allen Ginsberg, Lawrence Ferlinghetti, Gregory Corso), but there was also a long poem that he recited with extraordinary brio, even though he never mentioned the name of the author and the title. Later I found out that it was "Terrestris" by Ivan Blatný.

At the end of the 1970s, I began to publish a poetry series in *samizdat* with Vratislav Färber. The first author of the series was Zbyněk Hejda. Vráťa and I discussed with him which other authors would belong in the series. We agreed about the exilic work of Ivan Blatný—but the question was, how would we get access to those poems? After some time went by, Zbyněk asked me: "Would you still be interested in Blatný?" I answered in the affirmative. He showed me photocopies of a manuscript. The pages were not numbered, but there was a title page and a page with the date (November 2, 1979) and with a dedication to Gisèle Prassinos. It was obvious that it was a poetry collection. We agreed that we would not try to contact the poet—in order not to expose ourselves—and that we would publish *Bixley Remedial School* as we received it. We relied on our assumption of the poet's sanity, and it proved a good decision: Without the option of consulting with him, we learned to understand the peculiarities of his expression, and to respect them. Zbyněk lent me the manuscripts and I started transcribing them on the typewriter. We met often to discuss what I transcribed; we tried to decipher the hardly readable and incomprehensible places. We went through the "remedial school" of textology, history and culture. I learned a lot during this process, and I wrote a Master's thesis on the topic in 1998. I know of no other case when a manuscript was smuggled into Prague and came out in *samizdat* before *tamizdat*: At that time, manuscripts that could not be published in Czechoslovakia were smuggled out of Prague and into the West to be published.

Only after several years did Zbyněk Hejda tell us how Blatný's manuscript for *Bixley Remedial School* reached him. We were not surprised to learn that it was Jiří Kolář who had received it from Blatný. Like Blatný, Kolář also belonged to Group 42, which was more interested in testimony than in beauty. Kolář also knew about the selective (or manipulative) publishing of the manuscripts of some other Czech authors, including Ladislav Klíma and Karel Hynek Mácha. (Kolář published Mácha's complete diary in *samizdat*—including all of the portions that had been omitted from the officially

published "Complete Works").

Writing about *Old Addresses*—the collection of Blatný's poetry published in *tamiz-dat* in Toronto in 1979, which had been selected by its editor to include only the more traditional, accessible, monolingual poems from among Blatný's manuscripts —exiled critic Jiří Hron offered the following critique:

> [I]t was the duty of the editor to provide a more detailed description of the manuscripts ... Instead, what we learned from him was that "selecting ... proved in the end, to be quite a simple task." Of course it was an easy task, when he made it so easy for himself! As for what he did select ... the reader and the critic must consider it merely the first—and unfortunately an unreliable—glimpse into the creative, poetic, and human world of Ivan Blatný. For a more serious approach to the manuscripts, we still have to wait.[1]

I think that Kolář (who translated Eulenspiegel stories into Czech) understood the *tropos kynikos*[2] of *Bixley Remedial School*, and that through getting *Bixley* published he wanted to help the poet—this so-called mentally ill man—remedy the unreliability of *Old Addresses*. In an untitled prose poem, probably written in 1980,[3] Blatný makes his intention to resist beautification clear, by embracing the figure of the so-called degenerate artist:

> Ja, manchmal kann man wirkliche Gedichte schreiben, mit der geheimen Durst nach der schönen Kunst, so schön dass sogar Goebbels konnte sie rezitieren lassen auf einer Ausstellung der nicht entarteten Kunst. Auch so bleibe ich lustig, glücklich und entartet.[*] ... The silver spoon sugar competes with Tate and Lyle, yes Tate, and to Goebbels I must now say that I remain entartet.[†4]

Recently there was a premiere in Prague of a camerata opera based on the texts of Blatný's exilic poetry. It was called Kabaret Ivan Blatný. I was afraid that they would present the "unreliable" Blatný, but I gradually realized my fears were unfounded. The actor who played Blatný (the role was called "A man") started out wearing the "crazed" looks that inmates are sometimes portrayed with, and he slightly overplayed the stooped body posture that we know from the photographs of the elderly Blatný from the second half of the 1980s. But there were sparks gently blinking in his eyes. Repeatedly during the performance, a nurse would spread various pastes on the actor's face. But the pastes would fall off and disappear, especially when he stood up and sang with a full voice— and in these moments I found that "A man" corresponded to the opinion I had formed of Blatný over the years: a bright, joyous, resistive man. The actor, Karel Dobrý, is among

---

*Yes, sometimes one can write real poems, with a secret thirst for beautiful art, so beautiful that even Goebbels could allow them to be recited in an exhibition of non-degenerate art. Even so, I remain funny, happy and degenerate. (German)

†*entartete Kunst*: Degenerate art (German)

the best in our country. My fiancée remembered several of the melodies, and now she sings them around the flat, sometimes as she is working on Blatný's manuscripts. She especially likes the girl's aria based on Blatný's poem, "Goethe." The first two lines, sung in German, go like this: "Eine Verbeugung: Rosen spüren. / Die Freunde kommen zu gratulieren." Or, in English: "A bow: to sense roses. / Friends come to congratulate us."

I would like to congratulate Veronika, Matvei, and Anna for the idea of publishing Ivan's poems in New York. Thank you! Welcome to the remedial school.

—Antonín Petruželka
(translated by V. T.)

About this edition

FOR BLATNÝ'S POEMS from the 1940s, we have used the text from the Czech edition, *Ivan Blatný. Verše 1933-1953*. That collection, published in Brno in 1995, includes the contents of all four of Blatný's poetry books published before 1948 (*Paní Jitřenka, Melancholické procházky, Tento večer*, and *Hledání přítomného času*) and his two books of verse for children (*Jedna, Dvě, Tři, Čtyři, Pět* and *Na kopané*); it also contains poems published originally in newspapers, journals, and anthologies, some of Blatný's translations, and a selection of poems from manuscripts of the same period.

Two collections were published during Blatný's years in exile, *Stará bydliště* (*Old Addresses*) and *Pomocná škola Bixley* (*Bixley Remedial School*). Each has a specific publication history that must be addressed. In 1979, Sixty-Eight Publishers in Toronto published *Old Addresses*, edited by Antonín Brousek from manuscripts that were sent to him by Josef Škvorecký, who received them from Frances Meacham. Most of these poems were probably written in the 1970s, except for the poem "*Nokturno*," which was included in the anthology *Neviditelný domov* (*Invisible Home*), published in 1954 in Paris.

The same year *Old Addresses* appeared in Toronto, Blatný put together a collection which he titled *Bixley Remedial School*. It was brought to Prague from Paris by Erika Abrams, who got it from Jiří Kolář, and was published in *samizdat* in 1982 (under the imprint KDM, edited by Zbyněk Hejda, Antonín Petruželka and Vratislav Färber). Then, in 1987, Sixty-Eight Publishers published a book entitled *Bixley Remedial School*, edited by Brousek, which differed significantly from the 1982 *samizdat* edition. Brousek included more than twice as many texts in his edition, but extended Blatný's original title to refer to the entire book. Brousek indicates in the book's introduction that he worked with texts dating from 1979 to 1982. The poems Brousek chose to include in *Old Addresses* differ significantly from those in either version of *Bixley Remedial School*, although the material in these collections generally dates from the same period. For *Old Addresses*, Brousek selected poems that are formally more traditional than those in *Bixley*; there are very few multilingual poems. Blatný's own *Bixley Remedial School*, by contrast, includes a number of poems written entirely in English, and many poems in which he uses German and French.

For the present book, we have printed the poems from *Old Addresses* as they were published in 1997 and 2002 in Brno by Petrov, with an important exception: We have incorporated the corrections Blatný made on his typewritten proofs for the Toronto edition—corrections that did not make it into that book, or into any subsequent edition. (The reason for this is not clear: These authorial changes may have never reached

the editors or publishers of those volumes, or they may have been ignored.) The changes are as follows: In "*Cigareta*," *hřiště* has been changed to *hřííště*. In "*Fotbal*," *stíná* has been changed to *stírá* and *spad* has been changed to *spad'*. In "*Rýn*," the line that had been broken after "*obrostlé*" has been changed to break after "*hrady*"; in "*Nokturno*," the spelling of "*Morton-Marell*" has been corrected to "*Morton-Morell*," and the line that had been broken after "*vesnice*" has been changed to break after "*nezemře*." In the title of "*Hodiny vodné*" the word "*vodní*" has been changed into the Slovak "*vodné*." In "From a terrace in Prague," "Terrace" has been changed to "terrace" in the title; the line that had been broken after "*městě*" now breaks after "*obchodu*"; and the line that had been broken after "*to*" now breaks after "*terasy*."

For the poems from *Bixley Remedial School* we have used the text from the edition published by Torst in Prague in 1994. In our selection from this book, we have included many of the multilingual poems and poems written entirely in English, which we thought would be of interest to the English reader. The editors of the Prague volume of *Bixley Remedial School* (Antonín Petruželka, Zbyněk Hejda, and Vratislav Färber) made some changes to the poems, correcting what they determined to be "deviations from [Blatný's habitual] usage and the obvious errors." For this English edition we have followed their lead and have printed their versions of the poems. Their versions include the following "deviations" from Blatný's manuscript: In "*Léon-Paul Fargue*," *Léon Paul* was changed to *Léon-Paul*; in "*Janua Sapientiae*," "changeing" was changed to "changing"; in "*Pohřební hudba*," "knies" was changed to "knees"; in "*Tulák spí na louce*," "alway" was changed to "always"; in "Drink," "diseasis" was changed to "diseases"; in "*Systoly se napínají a povolují*," "*poměnky*" was changed to "*pomněnky*"; in "Outside and in," "linguiste" was changed to "linguist" and "to breath" was changed to "to breathe"; in "*Smutek*," "*Morgenstundeď*" was changed to "*Morgenstunden*"; in "Never light the job," "potatoe" was changed to "potato"; in "Happinesse," "happines" was changed to "happiness"; in "Misspelled," "unicorne" was changed to "unicorn"; in "*Cesta je poseta hvězdami*," "*sèmé d'étoile*" was changed to "*semée d'étoiles*." After collation with Blatný's manuscripts, two new changes were introduced (the first change was initiated during preparation for a forthcoming edition of *Bixley Remedial School* in Prague, and the second after collation in preparation for this edition): We changed "Felix slow" into "Felixtow" in the poem "Anarchy," and in the poem "Happinesse," we separated the last verse as a distinct strophe.

Thousands of pages were left after Blatný died in 1990; most are now in the Museum of National Literature in Prague (*Literární archiv PNP*). Many have been transcribed by a team of Czech scholars, but only a handful have been published to date. The last section of our book, "Another Poetical Lesson," benefits from this work. It includes

poems from manuscripts that have been published by Petruželka, Hejda, and Färber in Czech magazines as well as eight poems that appear here for the first time. The poems "Nížina," "High Class," "Ba Ba Black Sheep," and "Příroda" were published in *Revolver Revue* (Issue #47, 2001); "Come on you lazy censors," and "The end of Eternity" in *Literární noviny* (Issues #52-53, 2004); and "Another Poetical Lesson" in *A2* (Issue #12-13, 2005). The selection for this book was done by Veronika Tuckerová from the poems published in magazines and from about forty poems and prose texts which were transcribed from the manuscripts and made available, along with scans of the handwritten or typewritten originals, by Antonín Petruželka. Petruželka collated the poems. The poems in this section were either handwritten on hospital forms for "Job Costing details," or typed. Blatný probably wrote them at the same time as the poems from *Bixley Remedial School*, though some of them may have been written later. Blatný wrote during the day in a workshop he called "Pines" or "Hölderlin's workshop," where he had a typewriter at his disposal (albeit without the Czech diacritical marks). In the evenings and on the weekends he wrote in the Bixley Ward—in the television room, in the bathrooms, or on the bed.

In the previously published poems, we have retained the editorial decisions of Petruželka, Hejda, and Färber, and printed the poems as they were published in the aforementioned magazines: In "Nížina" we have retained the change from "returne" to "return"; in "High Class," we have retained the change from "moluscs" to "molluscs"; in "The end of Eternity," we have retained the changes from "sid" to "said" and "embarrassement" to "embarrassment." In the typewritten manuscript for "Come on you lazy censors" we have retained the change from *umrtnim* to *úmrtním,* in keeping with Blatný's practice of adding the correct diacritical marks to his poems typed on an English typewriter. We have also retained the change from "that s" to "that's" in "The end of Eternity." We have respected Blatný's usage of the initial lower case letter in the adjectives "czech," "english," and "hungarian." This is the Czech standard, which Blatný carried over into English. Blatný was generally consistent in his capitalization practice, adopting the Czech rule of distinguishing proper nouns by capitalizing them. So, although the title of his first collection of poems is *Paní Jitřenka*, Blatný uses *jitřenka* in the poem "La verre" (*Jitřenka* is the name for the morning star; a *jitřenka* is a neologism that could mean a woman who is stirred or roused, or who rouses another). What appear to be breaks from the standard norm for capitalization (e.g., "The end of Eternity" vs. "Another Poetical Lesson") we consider intentional on the author's part, and have retained. We are preserving Blatný's spelling of "oekology" (in "Another honor for my saint"), of "praepositions" (in "Both"), and of the German word "*eckelhaft*" (in "Příroda"), and the incorrect definite article "*das Glocke*" (in "Walter de la Mare"), all of which in our judgement may be

intentional. We have preserved the spelling of "dismanteled" in the poem "Walter de la Mare." We retain Blatný's usage of hyphenated words that are normally spelled without a hyphen: "gun-powder," "wheel-chair," "bee-hive." In "Ba, Ba, Black Sheep," Blatný enriches the English language with a neologism, "pendling": The Czech word "Pendlovat," which is etymologically related to "pendulum," means to move from one place to another and back, to commute.

In the poems that are published here for the first time, we have made only three changes to correct misspellings and typos: In "Bad Memory," "Drydens" has been changed to "Dryden's"; in "Queen, drones, bee-workers, život včel," "personelle" has been changed to "personnel" and "hives" to "hive's" (which could also have been changed to "hives'").

The poems in this section are written mostly in English; we would however like to point out that English poems do not outnumber Czech or multilingual ones in Blatný's exilic poetry (multilingual poems are the most frequent), and other languages are already present in some of Blatný's poems from the 1940s. In that respect, our decision to include a special section of poems in English for English speaking readers should not detract from the fact that the core of the poet's exilic writing is in the linguistically mixed poetry. Selections that do not take that into consideration are narrow; they are only parts that point to the whole.

—Veronika Tuckerová and Antonín Petruželka

Translators' notes

I WAS DRAWN to translate those parts of Blatný's œuvre that I most admire, i.e., the *Brno Elegies* (published under the title *Melancholické procházky* in 1941) and the formal poetry in the later work. For me these poems express most intensely and sharply Blatný's nostalgia for the land- and city-scapes around Brno. An expansive desire is barely contained in these poems: When he writes in later life from England, one understands this as the longing for the journey home, which is what nostalgia in its root sense is. It is curious then to witness him suffused by exactly that longing while still living and writing in Brno at the end of the 1930s and the beginning of the 1940s. The protectorate censor demanded that Blatný change his title from *Brno Elegies* to *Melancholy Walks*, concerned that the elegies might be construed as anti-occupation. But the emotions expressed in Blatný's elegies dwarf small brief events like the Third Reich, and range through Brno, the world, the universe and, most of all, and most hugely, the human soul in their midst.

I attempted, at nearly all costs, to maintain the rhyme of the originals, while adapting the meter from alexandrine to iambic pentameter. (The alexandrine meter is extremely unwieldy in English, but more importantly, the alexandrine meter in Czech has roughly the same prosodic valency as iambic pentameter. If Blatný had been writing in English, it is my belief that he would have used this classic meter.) My only justification for this is the belief that poetry is not primarily made up of images and ideas, but of words, and therein is the pattern of the soul. I also had a strong sense that Blatný comes home, as it were, in English translation. So although his work is suffused with the place names of Brno, along with its forgotten football players and teams, they belong in English as much as in Czech; Blatný insured this with his life.

My thanks to Tereza Límanová for her invaluable help with these translations.

—Justin Quinn

I KNEW NEXT to nothing about Ivan Blatný when I began to translate "The Game." Veronika Tuckerová had asked me if I'd be interested in translating something for an anthology of Blatný's works to be published by a small independent press in Brooklyn called Ugly Duckling. That was enough for me.

Veronika mailed me a longish prose poem with a 500-word-or-so biography of

Blatný enclosed. Of course I had heard of Blatný during the years I lived in Prague (which was where I began to translate professionally). I knew of *Skupina 42*, and while in Prague, I almost surely read some poems by members of the group, perhaps even some by Blatný himself. But that was it. What I discovered when I read the text Veronika sent me was a poet of great fantasy, with a refined sense of absurdity and a great gusto for language.

I cannot claim to know what "The Game" "means." Nor do I care. Blatný, I'm sure, was willing to take the risk to leave it up to the reader to find meaning in his work—assuming, that is, that the reader wishes to do so—and I see no reason not to respect that choice.

What I can say is this. Clearly "The Game" reflects the time and place in which it was written: post–World War II Europe, a time and place of great uncertainty, of shifting political, economic, and military alliances, and, in Czechoslovakia, a time of life-altering upheaval—in February 1948, the year after Blatný wrote "The Game," the Communist Party seized control of the government. The rest you can Google.

One thing I have learned over the years, and in fact one of the reasons I love translating so much, is that every translation is like life: a search for meaning. A search for meaning that doesn't always lead to answers.

It was a privilege to be asked to translate this work. I hope you enjoy it.

—Alex Zucker
Cape Cod, Massachusetts
February 26, 2007

WHAT A PITY that I must die
after I have exhausted all the sources of poetry
couldn't it be after all eternal?
The dissatisfaction of decided can't be stood

These lines are taken from Blatný's *Bixley Remedial School* (the 1994 edition), a book Veronika Tuckerová, the editor of this volume, introduced to me shortly after my arrival to the Czech Republic in 1995. I had just come from the National Poetry Foundation in Orono, Maine, to accept a job as English editor at the publishing house where Veronika was also employed.

That book, a collection of pieces written in the late 1970s–early 1980s by Blatný in a British mental health care institution, is written in a mixture of English, Czech, German, and French: verse where languages intrude upon each other like Shakespeare's scene-stealing bit players. And phrases, too—scraps of memory, letters sent by friends, words caught from the television, newspapers, radio. Living as I was in a strange linguistic environment populated by false cognates, half-heard intrusions and other white noise, that book spoke to me; or, as we Americans say, I could relate. I wanted more and soon ordered a copy of Blatný's collected poems, *Verses* (*Verše*), through the publishing house machinery.

Reading the collected poems, I became aware of the early Blatný, the lovely lyrical work. Like Kundera, Blatný is a product of Brno, and his verse written in and about Brno remains important to the town. Blatný was born in 1919, practically coeval with the founding of Czechoslovakia. Brno was the second largest city in the country, the capital of Moravia, a growing metropolis finally out from under the vulture's wing of Vienna. It was a city of industry and business, but it was also a city of optimism: Without the historical weight of Prague, Brno was a city living for the present and excited about the future (beautifully expressed in its architecture). All of that was ruined by the Nazi occupation; that loss is palpable in Blatný's verse.

When my copy of *Verses* arrived in the office, I was greeted by my co-editors either with admiration (for trying to learn the language through Blatný's work), or derision (for trying to learn a language peculiar to Blatný alone). Later, when asking colleagues of mine at the Czech university where I teach for assistance with a difficult phrase, they simply shook their heads, muttering "*Blatnýština!*"—"Blatný-ese!"—and walked away.

In my experience, there seems to be little middle ground in the appreciation of Blatný's work. It's not hard to see why. Passages like the one quoted above can present problems for readers—the elegiac feelings of the first three lines seem thwarted by the syntactic problems of the fourth, a knot that cannot be untied easily, if at all.

Not surprisingly, whatever difficulties *Blatnýština* presents to the reader are only magnified for the translator. But that is not a bad thing: Exactly where translation is difficult is where language is doing something interesting, original. Translators of poor verse or prose (or of a poor line or weak phrase) are often faced with a dilemma: Translate "faithfully," or make it better. A bad sentence translated accurately can just look like a bad translation.

But for translators of difficult verse it is important to convey that difficulty, those convolutions of the gray matter parleyed with much hair twisting into curves of ink on paper. I believe that if something is easy, it's no fun; and I've had a lot of fun pulling my hair, trying to render *Blatnýština* into Blatnýese. I'm glad that Ugly Duckling Presse has

printed Ivan Blatný's work here in the original, too, and my hope is that our English versions will help to draw more readers (and readers who are writers) to focus their attention on his poetic experiments.

My thanks to the editors of previous editions of Blatný's work for making him available, and to the editors of this volume, who have been both extremely diligent and accommodating. My thanks to Veronika, for 12 years of friendship and guidance.

And to first-time readers of Blatný, I say this: The satisfaction of undecided can be stood.

—Matthew Sweney, Olomouc, 2007

THE TASK OF rendering Blatný's multilingual poems "into English" is, obviously, a challenging one. The questions begin immediately: What would constitute an English translation of a poem, when the linguistic makeup of the original is 75% Czech, 20% English and 5% other? Do these poems resist translation so much they refute it? If not, then how should one proceed? Which parts should be translated? Every word in a language other than English? Only the Czech? And how, in the translated text, can the portions that were written in English be identified for the new reader?

For this volume, the last of these issues was addressed in the typesetting: Portions of the poems that have not been changed appear in gray type in the translations, at the very least alerting the reader to a distinction between the lines that have been translated and those that are Blatný's own. But in addition to this purely indexical function, we hope that the bicolor appearance will also serve as a reminder that these poems don't lend themselves to a conventional understanding of translation as the transmission of a text from one language to another. Here the transmission is interrupted before it can go through: The gray type is really 40% black—a black that is holding back. The typesetting makes another subtle gesture: In this section of the book, originals are printed above the translations, in an attempt to coerce every reader—not just those with an interest in the Czech language, whose eye is already turned toward the verso in the facing-page format—to take in the original first.

"Take in," rather than read, because to a certain extent these poems resist our usual reading habits as much as they resist conventions of translation. A poem in which the first six lines, written in Czech, are followed by a couplet reading "The guest star is Bing Crosby / the guest star is Bob Hope" provides one set of delights to a non-Czech-speaking reader and another to a Czech reader who may not know English but may nonetheless recognize the names of Crosby and Hope. And in the bilingual poem "The Last

Poem October 18th," the two English lines that poke through the Czech—"I have now two pens and plenty of papers" and "dark green ivy is overgrowing the vicarage"—seem to form their own conversation, which encourages even a Czech-ignorant reader to pick out overtones in the surrounding sea of language, for instance picking out "ink" from the nearby word, *inkoust*. Of course, the experience of a Czech reader is completely different—the inverse, perhaps—and that of the bilingual reader is something else, too.

Those who feel that the goal of translation is strictly to recreate the effect of a text in a new context (for a new audience) might recommend the "compensatory" strategy of reversing the lines that are in Czech and English—that is, translating lines originally written in English into Czech, in an attempt to approximate the effect of the poems on a Czech speaker. But, though this would be amusing and might result in interesting poetry, to do so here would be to misunderstand Blatný's poetics. The foreign words and phrases he uses are not there simply as other, separate but equal modes of expression, nor are they mere decoration. They are "insertions," valuable in themselves and not only for their meaning—like scraps of newspaper pasted into a collage.

Blatný's native tongue was Czech and he lived for decades surrounded by English; the other languages that are present in these poems are there much more occasionally. For this reason, and also to preserve a bit of the feeling of a collage even in our translations, we have left the third and fourth languages (German and French) untranslated, even in our English versions (though translations of these lines do appear in end-notes).

Is it any more impossible (or possible, for that matter) to translate multilingual poems than any others? In writing Blatný's Czech into English, we encountered the usual obstacles as we attempted to render tone, meaning, and music, while honoring the word-play of which Blatný was so fond. If anything, we had a rare luxury: In the case of many poems, after we had gotten just a few words as right as we could, our job was done.

—Anna Moschovakis and Veronika Tuckerová

Notes to the text

Introduction

1. Ivan Blatný, *Pomocná škola Bixley*, eds. Antonín Petruželka, Zbyněk Hejda, and Vratislav Färber (Prague: KDM, 1982).

2. A book of his exilic poetry, *Old Addresses* (*Stará bydliště*), had been published in Toronto in 1979.

3. In 1968, his second book of poetry, *Melancholy Walks* (*Melancholické procházky*), was republished by Blok in Brno in a limited special edition to mark the new year.

4. Signed "*Břz.*" [Bohuslav Březovský] in "Český básník?", *Národní osvobození* (March 31, 1948). Quoted in *Ivan Blatný. Texty a dokumenty, 1930-1948* (Brno: Atlantis, 1999). 347. Translation of all quotations from *Ivan Blatný. Texty a dokumenty*: Veronika Tuckerová.

5. Signed "*ok.*" [Oldřich Kryštofek], "Pospíšil si." *Mladá fronta* (April 2, 1948). Quoted in *Ivan Blatný. Texty a dokumenty*. 356.

6. *Ivan Blatný. Texty a dokumenty*. 345.

7. *Ivan Blatný. Texty a dokumenty*. 346, 355.

8. A 1954 diagnosis of paranoid schizophrenia is reported in *Texty a dokumenty* (453). Jürgen Serke also addresses the topic in "Útěk do blázince" ("Escape into Madhouse"), an interview/article republished (from *Stern* magazine) in *Pomocná škola Bixley* (Praha: KDM, 1982). Serke writes that though Blatný's chart at St. Clement's described a number of Blatný's defects, they were generally attributed to possible rather than exact diagnoses. (*Pomocná škola Bixley*. 180)

9. Petruželka, "Básník Mlok a poetika dokumentu." *Souvislosti*, Vol. 16, No. 3, (2005): 147-158.

10. *Pomocná škola Bixley*. 178-182.

11. *Ivan Blatný. Texty a dokumenty*. 453.

12. *Pomocná škola Bixley*. 180-181. Another argument for Blatný's sanity is made by Petruželka in "Básník Mlok a poetika dokumentu": The secret agent who was sent to visit Blatný at Claybury Hospital was a medical doctor by profession and an old friend of Blatný's from Brno who presumably would not raise his suspicion. His mission was to inquire about the poet's current health and mental state (as well as his legal status in Britain) and to gently convince Blatný to return to Czechoslovakia—where the secret police hoped they could persuade the poet to write a propagandistic book reporting the "real situation of the exiles." The agent's report on his visit to Blatný reiterates the poet's claim that he was satisfied in the asylum. The agent's conclusion was that even had Blatný decided to return, Czechoslovakia could not use him for propagandistic purposes. Petruželka concludes that the secret police reports unwittingly attest to Blatný's sanity, showing that the poet understood the situation very well and was not a victim of paranoia. Petruželka also raises a number of questions about the reliability of this particular agent's report: What to make of his conclusion that Blatný was mentally ill, but that his illness could be cured by "the opposite factors of those that caused it"? Had he been forced to collaborate against his will? Had he tried to protect Blatný by warning him that the secret police was after him?

13. Martin Pluháček, "Ivan Blatný," published as an Afterword in *Stará bydliště* (Brno: Petrov, 1992).

14. Five of Blatný's poems were included in the anthology *Neviditelný domov: Verše exulantů 1948-1953* (*Invis-*

ible Home: The Verses of the Exiled, 1948-1953), ed. Peter Demetz (Paris: Sokolova, 1954).

15. Zbyněk Hejda, "Passer-By. The Poetry of Ivan Blatný," *Metre 12* Autumn (2002): 182. Translation: Justin Quinn.

16. Šmarda's recollections of his visits to his cousin can be found in his article, "Život pro poezii" ("Life for Poetry") in *Universitas. Vol.* 23/6 (1990): 16-20.

17. Most of the manuscripts wound up in a Jesuit institution called Velehrad in London. They were acquired after the revolution by the Archives of the Museum of National Literature in Prague.

18. The textual history of both collections is discussed in detail by Antonín Petruželka, in "Pomocná škola Bixley jako textologický a ediční problém," *Kritický sborník.* Vol. 18 (1998/1999), no. 1 (Fall 98): 36-59.

19. Ivan Blatný, *Verše 1933-1953*, ed. Rudolf Havel. (Brno: Atlantis, 1995). 595.

20. From an unpublished poem, "The Languages."

21. This observation was made by Jiří Trávníček in "Pod sankcí paměti," in *Poezie poslední možnosti* (Prague: Torst, 1996). 173-174.

22. "Jsem jenom básník jednoho jazyka," in *Pomocná škola Bixley* (1994). 97.

23. The position of Czech and English in Blatný's poetry is discussed in "Pod sankcí paměti" by Trávníček, who argues that Czech remains Blatný's stronger language—the language of memory, depth and poetry—while English is the language of surface, exterior occurance, linearity, and taboo. Petruželka suggests the contrary, that Czech may have lost its exclusive position in Blatný's exilic poetry. In Petruželka's view, Blatný may have gained the freedom to write not from the "perspective of one dominant language," but in the "quiet opposition toward any standard usages or partial perspective." Blatný's poetics, based originally in one exclusive language, became more than a "mosaics of languages." Blatný liberated poetry from its "monoglotic" foundation and based it elsewhere, so the reader can "catch and respect a number of different perspectives." Antonín Petruželka, "Němčina, Němci a němota v poetice Ivana Blatného." (Může být jazyk básně předjazykový a necizí?) [German, Germans and muteness in the poetics of Ivan Blatný. Can the language of a poem be pre-lingual and non-alien?]. *Souvislosti.* 16/3 (2005): 147-158. Translation: Veronika Tuckerová.

24. Zbyněk Hejda, "Passer-By. The Poetry of Ivan Blatný." 174.

25. "Hradečný ke mně blíže," *Pomocná škola Bixley* (1994). 81.

26. Antonín Brousek, "Návrat ztraceného básníka," *Podřezávání větve* (Prague: Torst, 1999). 470-473. First published as the Epilogue to *Stará bydliště* (Toronto: Sixty-Eight publishers, 1979). Translation: Veronika Tuckerová.

27. Other members of Group 42 included the poets Jan Hanč, Jiřina Hauková, and Josef Kainar; visual artists František Gross, František Hudeček, Jan Kotík, Kamil Lhoták, Bohumír Matal, Jan Smetana, Karel Souček, Miroslav Hák, Ladislav Zívr, and theoretician Jiří Kotalík.

28. Jindřich Chalupecký, "Svět, v němž žijeme," published in 1940. As quoted in *Obhajoba umění 1934-1948*, (Prague: Československý spisovatel, 1991). 71, 73. Translation: Veronika Tuckerová.

29. The intertextual relationship between Blatný and the poets Langston Hughes and Milada Součková is the topic of an essay by Julia Hansen, "Singing the blues: Intertextuality in the poetry of Ivan Blatný," published in *Kosmas: Czechoslovak and Central European Journal* Vol. 16, no. 1 (Fall 2002): 21-36.

FROM BRNO ELEGIES

pp 1-9 The addressee of these poems is male, a fact that is necessarily lost in English translation.

FROM THIS NIGHT

p. 19 *Druhá*: feminine form of the word "second."

p. 25 F.H.: the artist František Hudeček (1909-1990).

FROM IN SEARCH OF PRESENT TIME

p. 33 The Paris Peace Conference (in September 1945) discussed important post-war issues, such as the establishment of post-war states and the deportation of ethnic Germans from Central Europe.

p. 37 *Druhý*: Masculine form of the word "second."

This poem was first published under the title "*Zpěv*" ("Song").

Mi estas esperantisto! Parolu esperante, Ivano!: "I am an Esperantist! Speak Esperanto, Ivan!" (Esperanto). Esperantists were sent to the Nazi concentration camps for being internationalists.

p 41 Coprophags: beings that eat feces.

p.47 Caelia was a Fairy Queen in the Arthurian Legends. Tom a'Lincoln, King Arthur's bastard son, was her lover. She committed suicide by drowning herself.

FROM THE GAME

p. 63 *An die Muse*: "To the muse." (German)

Was ich ohne dich wäre, ich weiss es nicht—aber mir grauet, / seh' ich, was ohne dich Hundert' und Tausende sind.: "What would I be without you? I know not—but I tremble / on seeing what hundreds and thousands of men are without you." (German)

p. 63 *André Chénier hat dem ewigen Geklapper des Alexandriners ein Ende bereitet.:* "André Chénier has laid to rest the never-ending tintamar of alexandrine verse." (German)

das ewige Geklapper des dem ewigen Geklapper des Alexandriners ein Ende bereitetenden André Chénier.: "The never-ending tintamar of André Chénier laying to rest the never-ending tintamar of alexandrine verse." (German)

FROM OLD ADDRESSES

p. 73 Antonin Chittussi (1847-1891): Czech Impressionist landscape painter.

p. 77 Brušák: Karel Brušák (1913-2004): Czech exile poet.

Listopad: František Listopad (1921-): Czech exile poet.

Dresler: Jaroslav Dresler (1925-1999): Czech exile poet.

p. 95 Milada Součková (1899-1983): poet and writer; wife of the artist Zdeněk Rykr (1901-1940) who was admired by the members of Group 42.

p. 97 *Stimmung*: "mood" (German)

Žabovřesky is a suburb of Blatný's native Brno, but it also has a connotation in Czech akin to "Podunk" in American English.

from Bixley Remedial School

p. 106 *Der Dichter spricht in verschiedenen Sprachen:* "The poet speaks in various languages" (German) *wie:* "how" (German).

p. 107 *Wiesen:* "meadows" (German)

p.111 *muchachas:* "friends" (Spanish)

p.119 *Einsames Bett, traurige Morgenstunden, / die schöne Hochzeit ist verschwunden.:* "Lonely bed, sad morning hours, / the beautiful wedding disappeared." (German)

Another Poetical Lesson

p.133 *Paní Jitřenka* was the title of Blatný's first book (1940).

Svatopluk Kadlec (1898-1971): poet and translator, e.g., of Baudelaire.

Valentine Penrose (1898-1978): Surrealist painter and novelist.

p. 141 "Pendling" is a neologism possibly derived from *pendlovat,* a Czech word that means to move from one place to another, to commute.

Rosa Bonheur (1822-1899): French painter and sculptor.

p. 151 John Dryden's poem "Annus Mirabilis" (1667) was written while the poet was living in Wiltshire, having removed himself from London to escape the Great Plague. The title means "year of miracles" and the poem refers to dramatic events in 1666 (including the Battle of Lowestoft and the Great Fire of London) in which the poet saw averted disasters.

p. 153 Walter John de la Mare (1873-1956): English poet, short story writer, and novelist, known for his works for children.

Afterword

1. Jiří Hron, "Mírně řečeno: o nepřesnosti," *Listy 10,* říjen č. 5 (1980): 48-49.

2. *Tropos kynikos:* literally, "cynical mode" (Greek). This concept, central to the influential 1998 Peter Steiner essay, "*Tropos Kynikos: The Good Soldier Švejk* by Jaroslav Hašek" refers to the intentionally "confusing," resistive linguistic behavior of the Greek *kynik* (cynic) philosopher, Diogenes of Sinope—a semiotic self-defence that subverts the ideas of power and truth via the slippage of linguistic signs. ("*Tropos Kynikos: The Good Soldier Švejk* by Jaroslav Hašek" in Peter Steiner, *The Deserts of Bohemia: Czech fiction and its social context.* New York: Cornell University Press, 2000.)

3. "Úvoz je příliš hluboké údolí", typewritten 6-A-5 7, probably from the year 1980; published in *Literární noviny* 52-53 (2004): 31

4. Joseph Goebbels, Adolf Hitler's Propaganda Minister in Nazi Germany, was also a poet.

Books by Ivan Blatný

Paní Jitřenka. Prague: Melantrich, 1940. In the series *Poezie*.

Melancholické procházky. Prague: Melantrich, 1941. In the series *Poezie*.

Tento večer. Prague: B. Stýblo, 1945. In the series *Knižnice Lyra*. With illustrations by Kamil Lhoták.

Na kopané. Blansko: Karel Jelínek, 1946. Illustrations by Kamil Lhoták. In the series *Prvosenka*.

Hledání přítomného času. Prague: Mladá fronta, Práce and Svoboda, 1947.

Jedna, dvě, tři, čtyři, pět. Prague: F. Borový, 1947. Illustrations by Kamil Lhoták.

Stará bydliště. Toronto: Sixty-Eight Publishers, 1979. ed. Antonín Brousek.

Pomocná škola Bixley. Prague: Kde domov můj, 1982. eds. Zbyněk Hejda, Vratislav Färber, Antonín Petruželka. (*Samizdat*.)

Pomocná škola Bixley. Toronto: 68 Publishers, 1987. ed. Antonín Brousek. (Different selection from the 1982/1994 book of the same name.)

Stará bydliště. Brno: Petrov, 1992/1997/2002.

Tento večer. Praha: Československý spisovatel, 1993. Selected by Jan Maria Tomeš.

Pomocná škola Bixley, 2nd edition: Prague: Torst, 1994.

Verše 1933-1953. Brno: Atlantis, 1995. ed. Rudolf Havel.

Jsem nyní se všemi. Brno: Petrov, 1998. ed. Martin Reiner.

Brněnské elegie. Prague: BB Art, 2003. Selected by Zdeněk Hron.

Fragmenty a jiné verše z pozůstalosti. Host, 2003. Selected and edited by Jan Šmarda.

Poèmes. Alfortville: Editions Revue K, 1989. Translated into French by Erika Abrams.

Le Passant. Paris: Orphée/La Différence, 1992. ed. Zbyněk Hejda.Translated into French by Erika Abrams.

Landschaft der neuen Wiederholungen. C. Weihermüller, 1992. Translated into German by Radim Klekner.

Szkoła specjalna. Wiersze wybrane. Kraków-Warszawa: Biblioteka L.E., 1993. Translated into Polish by Leszek Engelking.

U podrazi za sadašnim vremenom. Beograd: Pismo, 1997. Translated into Serbian by Biserka Rajčić.

Hilfsschule Bixley. Klagenfurt: Wieser, 2002. Translated into German by Christa Rothmeier.

Alte Wohnsitze. Wien: Edition Korrespondenzen, 2005. Translated into German by Christa Rothmeier.

Acknowledgments

The many people who helped make this book possible are thanked by the editors and translators in their notes. Ugly Duckling Presse is grateful to the New York State Council on the Arts for its support of the Eastern European Poets Series, and to the National Endowment for the Arts for helping to fund this book. UDP would also like to thank the editors of the *Harvard Review, Ygdrasil,* and *Action Yes,* in which some of the poems and translations in this book first appeared.